Angels,
Teddy Bears,
and Roses

DEBORAH NORTON

Angels, Teddy Bears, and Roses
by Deborah Norton

Printed in South Carolina, in the United States of America

Unless otherwise indicated, Bible quotations are taken from *The New International Version.* Copyright © 1973 by International Bible Society, Colorado Springs, Colorado.

Cover Design by Narrow Way Design

ISBN-13: 978-1493530854
ISBN-10: 1493530852

DEDICATION

In Memory of my Dear Foster Mother

Mary S. Blackstock

04/24/1911 ~ 05/02/1986

ACKNOWLEDGMENTS

I would like to express my deepest gratitude to friend and fellow author, Jeanie Cline, for her support and encouragement throughout the writing and publication of this book.

I would also like to thank my family for lovingly putting up with my absence while I spent that time away from them writing.

May God bless and keep you all in His Love and Grace.

PROLOGUE

To look at Madge Denning you would never know she could hate one of her own children. She was beautiful. Ebony hair, porcelain skin, and emerald green eyes were a constant draw to every man who saw her. Having five children was the result of that beauty. Not having a husband was the result of her temperament. Each child had a different father. Each father was a soldier and none of them stuck around long enough to know the children.

Struggling to raise them all, Madge did what she did best to bring home a meager living. She became a prostitute.

She named her firstborn, Rocky because his father talked about living in the rugged Rocky mountains. Dakota's father was from Fargo. She decided to name the rest of the children with names she simply liked - Stevie, Brenden and Alysa.

Although she would never say so, Dakota was the child she hated.

CHAPTER ONE

Late summer of 1963 should have been a carefree, happy time for eleven-year-old Dakota but the sweltering South Carolina heat silenced even her. The tomboy longed to be in her favorite tree. Instead, she daydreamed of exploring the White Horse Canyons near her grandmother's house. Naturally shy, unimposing and introverted, she absolutely loved books and daydreaming.

"Dakota!" Mama barked, shattering her afternoon dreams. "What are you doing?" Mama's accusatory tone put Dakota on alert.

"I was just about to come see if you want something to drink," Dakota lied. She ran to the living room.

"Where are the boys?" Mama asked.

"I don't know." Dakota shrugged and tossed her long pigtails over her shoulders.

"Well, check on them, stupid!" Mama didn't have an ounce of patience. "Then get in that kitchen and make us some lunch."

"Yes, Mama."

Dakota came back a few minutes later with a plate and a glass of lemonade.

Mama dabbed her handkerchief at the sweat tickling her temple. "What is this?" she asked in disgust. She fingered the sandwich on the plate, then picked it up and threw it at Dakota. "What *is* that?"

"A mayonnaise sandwich," the girl replied.

"Have you lost your mind, Dakota? Get in there and fix me something decent for lunch!"

Dakota shuffled toward the door. "It's...it's all we have, Mama. You want me to call Mama Mary and ask her to bring us some food?"

Mama's temper exploded as she jumped up from the couch. "No, I don't want you to call Mary," she said, mocking her. "Mary is not your mama, I am! You watch the kids and I'll go get us some food."

Dakota's brown eyes widened with fear as Mama pushed her to the side on her way out. She tip-toed to the back of the house to check on two-year-old Alysa. Dakota hoped the baby would sleep until Mama came back. Then she remembered Rocky was playing basketball at T.J.'s. *Now where did the other two sneak off to?* she wondered. She made her way back to the kitchen and saw eight-year-old Stevie and seven-year-old Brenden through smudged glass on the back door. They were running through the yard. *Now is my chance,* she thought. The rotary dial had never been so slow. "Mama Mary?" she whispered into the phone as she heard the ringing stop.

"Hey sweetheart," Mary answered.

"Mama Mary, I'll probably get into trouble for calling you. Mama hates me and she told me not to call. But we don't have any food and I told her you would bring us some but she just got mad and..." Dakota heard a noise behind her. She turned expecting to see blond-haired Alysa. It was Mama!

"I have to go now," the girl said, and slammed down the phone.

Mama back-handed Dakota so hard, the child fell to the floor with a thump. Dakota knew what was coming. She was used to Mama beating her but that didn't lessen the pain.

"I told you not to call her," Mama said through clenched teeth.

"Please, Mama," Dakota begged. She began to whimper. "Please, don't. I won't do it again."

Madge fell to the floor with Dakota. Straddling her daughter, she sat on Dakota's stomach. Choking her with her left hand, she balled her right hand into a fist and began hitting Dakota's face. The child fought back, kicking and screaming. The last thing Dakota saw before blacking out was Mama's enraged face.

When Dakota awoke, Stevie was sitting on the

floor looking at her. "What did you do this time?" he asked.

Stevie loved Dakota. He was always coming to her rescue. But then he was always rescuing something...frogs, cats, baby birds. Stevie had liquid blue eyes and a marshmallow heart. "Can you see?" he asked her.

Dakota's eyes were swollen almost shut. "I can see," Dakota told him. "But my face hurts something awful. She struggled to get up and Stevie helped her.

"Mama left," Stevie said.

"I called Mary," Dakota told him. "It made her real mad."

Mary and Mama had a long history together. They had been best friends for years. Dakota knew something had happened to tear them apart. Mary and her husband, Dave, could not have children of their own, so they loved everyone else's. They especially loved Dakota.

Whenever Madge needed a babysitter, Mary was there. For eleven years Mary had helped raise Dakota. Now, the only time Madge would have anything to do with Mary was in an emergency.

Dakota often wondered how the two had become best friends. They were total opposites. In contrast to Mama's beauty, Mary was just plain. She was short and round with faded blue eyes and impossible hair. But her touch, voice and demeanor were so gentle, Dakota thought she was the most beautiful person on earth. Mary told Dakota many times, "Pretty comes from the inside."

Dakota looked a lot like Mama but she felt ugly. Now, she remembered Mary's words as she looked at her swollen, bruised face in the mirror. *I'll have to skip school tomorrow*, she thought. *Mrs. Cleveland will have a fit!*

As the bell rang at school the next day, Mary knocked on Mrs. Cleveland's door. The grey haired teacher settled her sixth grade class, then invited Mary to speak in the hallway. This was not the first time both women were concerned about Dakota.

"She isn't here, is she?" Mary asked.

"No," Mrs. Cleveland replied. "Has something happened?"

"I suspect so," Mary told her. "She called yesterday but hung up in a hurry. She was afraid of getting into trouble. She said there was no food in the house."

"That poor, sweet girl." Mrs. Cleveland sighed. "I have asked her so many times to tell me about her bruises and every time she comes up with a different story. Either she ran into a cabinet door, or she fell off the porch, or she was playing football with her brothers. I think she's just too scared to tell me the truth. I've thought about calling the police to see if they can get her to tell about those bruises."

"I doubt that would do any good," Mary said. "Madge is friendly with just about every policeman down there."

Mrs. Cleveland shook her head in disbelief. "I'll let you know when she comes back to school."

"Thank you," said Mary.

That afternoon, Mrs. Cleveland pulled into the parking lot of the local five and dime. She watched in disbelief as a police officer helped Dakota into the back of a patrol car. She parked quickly and jumped from her station wagon calling out to the officer.

"Please! Wait! Why on earth are you putting her in there?"

"Do you know this girl?"

"Yes," replied Mrs. Cleveland. "She is one of my pupils."

"Well, one of your pupils is about to learn a lesson about shoplifting," the officer told her.

Mrs. Cleveland edged closer to the black and white sedan. She looked inside and gasped when she saw Dakota's face. "Looks like shoplifting is the least of this child's problems. This girl has been beaten."

"Now hold on," the officer said in a lazy southern drawl. "I've already asked her about the black eyes. She said she got into a fight with her brother and the brother won."

Mrs. Cleveland crossed her arms and looked at him in disbelief. "You don't really believe that, do you?" she asked.

"Well, that's what she said happened, so why shouldn't I believe her?"

"What was she trying to steal?" Mrs. Cleveland

waited for an answer.

"Makeup," he mumbled.

"What?"

The officer spoke up. "Liquid makeup. She said she needed it to cover up the bruises."

Raising her brow, Mrs. Cleveland gave him an '*I told you so*' look. "What will happen to her now?" she inquired.

"I'll be taking her home and talking to her parents."

"Good luck with that," she told him.

The teacher then went home to call Mama Mary.

As the police car pulled into Madge Denning's driveway, brown-haired Stevie jumped up from the *pretend fort* he was building in the dirt. He ran inside the little yellow house.

"Mama! Mama!" he cried. "The police are here!" His screaming startled Alysa and the girl began to cry. Brenden ran to the door getting in front of Madge causing her to curse. "What now?" she said under her breath. As Madge talked to the policeman, she was cordial and almost syrupy sweet but as soon as he pulled out of the driveway, Dakota watched Mama's face change.

She grabbed Dakota by the arm and pulled her inside the house.

"Rocky," Mama called. "Bring me the belt."

Fourteen-year-old Rocky did as he was told. He then picked up Alysa and left the room. Stevie and Brenden followed him - Stevie already covering his ears.

The belt was a three inch wide strap of leather with a heavy metal buckle on the end. It was a man's belt. Dakota didn't know which man it had come from but she hated him.

"Turn around," Mama ordered.

Dakota turned and flinched as the first strike of the belt hit her back. This time she didn't try to fight back. She had no strength left. She had missed the meal at school that usually kept her going. She fell to her knees and laid her head on the couch protecting her head with her arms. Her body racked with sobs as Mama left welt after welt.

The next two weeks were a blur for Dakota. The doctor at the free clinic said it was the flu. He wasn't concerned about the bruises saying most kids get them. Dakota was weak and feverish and all she wanted to do was sleep. On top of that, the doctor said as soon as Dakota was strong enough he was going to put her in the hospital to take out her tonsils.

It was almost more than Mama could take. She had lost her housekeeper, her cook, and her babysitter, all in one fell swoop. She gave in and did what she hated to do. She called Mary.

"Hello?"

"Hello, Mary?" Mama asked.

"Hello, Madge. I heard Dakota has been real sick. How is she?"

"That's why I'm calling," Mama told her. She

then proceeded to explain that Dakota would be laid up for awhile. "I can't take care of her and four other kids and work every night."

"I didn't know you were working now," Mary said. "Where at?"

"Cocktail waitress at the Oasis Club," Mama replied. "The welfare check just ain't enough." Mary knew Mama was lying but she played along.

"Anyway, I hate to ask you," Mama said, "but can you take Dakota for awhile?"

"I'll do anything I can to help," Mary said. "Do you need me to come get her?"

Mama hated to let Dakota go to Mary's. But she hated taking care of her more.

"Yes, come get her."

Children are a heritage from the Lord, offspring a reward from Him. Psalm127:3

CHAPTER TWO

Mary stopped at the store to stock up on aspirin, juice, and chicken soup. Then she went to get Dakota. She was shocked when she saw Dakota. The child was naturally long and lanky but now she was so thin Mary was able to pick her up and carry her to the car. Dakota's round, brown eyes were now closed in exhausted sleep. "My poor, sweet baby," Mary whispered. "Mama Mary and the good Lord is going to get you better."

For several days Mary spoon fed Dakota. She sponge bathed her and gently nursed her, replenishing her strength.

One afternoon Dakota awoke to a soft, fuzzy teddy bear lying beside her. Dakota looked around the room, happy to realize she was at Mama Mary's house. This had been her room for as long as she could remember. She lay in the white canopy bed and admired the teddy bears sitting all around the room. Large and small, brown and white, she loved each one. Mary walked in just as Dakota pulled the newest bear close, snuggling against its warm, brown fur.

"Well," Mary said. "I see you found your new friend."

"Hey, Mama Mary." Dakota sat up, arms outstretched. "Thank you for my new teddy bear," she said as she hugged the robust woman.

"You're welcome, honey." Mary hugged her back, then placed her hand on Dakota's forehead. "You feeling better?"

"Yes, ma'am, Mama Mary. I wish you was my real mama. I wish I could live with you all the time."

Mary sat on the side of the bed. "I wish you could too, sweetie. But you know your Mama won't let you."

"I don't know why," Dakota replied. "If she hates me so much, why does she want me there?"

Mary knew the answer to that. She knew Madge's welfare check would be cut back but she didn't say so.

"Dave will be home soon. Feel like sitting in the kitchen with us for supper?"

A booming voice came from the doorway. "Of course she does," Dave said.

"Big Daddy!" Dakota cried. "I haven't seen you in so long!"

Dave came to her bedside. "Big Daddy has

missed you too," he said and planted a kiss on the top of her head.

Dave was a big man. He stood over six feet tall with broad shoulders and a strong back. Because of his Native American heritage his skin was deeply stained and his wavy hair jet black. He was big and strong but Dakota knew he was as gentle as the teddy bear in her arms.

The following day, it was time for Dakota to go to the hospital. She was scared. Mary calmed her and explained as much as she could of what would happen. Dakota felt better about it when she found out she could have all the ice cream she wanted once the operation was done.

"Can I come back home with you?" she asked Mary.

"Yes, for awhile," Mary answered.

Three days after her tonsils were removed, Dakota declared she never wanted another bowl of ice cream. "Can I have a bowl of Big Daddy's oyster stew?" she asked. "He makes the best."

She healed, gained weight, and Mary helped her catch up on her school work.

Soon it was time for Dakota to go back home. She cried all the way there. Mary pulled her Buick to the side of the road before reaching Madge's house. Taking Dakota in her arms she tried to console her. "If you need me, call."

Mary thought about how it had been three

weeks since Dakota came to stay with her, and Madge had not called to check on her once.

"Wait a minute, Mama Mary," Dakota requested. Quickly, the girl jumped from the car. There were pink wild roses growing on the embankment. Carefully, Dakota broke three stems trying to avoid the thorns.

She jumped back into the car shoving the roses at Mary. "You're always giving me Teddy Bears," she said, "so I will give you roses."

Mary smiled and held the roses all the way to Madge's house and then all the way home.

Dakota was glad to see her siblings running to greet her. She had missed them. They bombarded her with questions about the surgery. Dakota noticed that Mama didn't have much to say and then a feeling of dread came over her.

Her first night home was a cold one. Summer was giving way to fall. The days were hot but tonight there was a chill in the air. The big, brown heater in the living room did a good job of heating the front part of the house but little of it reached the bedrooms. It was midnight when Dakota placed a blanket on the hardwood floor in front of the fan blowing out the warm air. Madge didn't like it when Dakota did this but Dakota was cold.

Maybe Mama won't wake up, Dakota thought. *Maybe she won't know.*

At two o'clock a.m., Mama came in the front door almost tripping over the girl sleeping soundly on her blanket.

"Idiot girl," Mama mumbled. She stepped to the corner of the room and grabbed the broom leaning on the wall. Whoosh!

With one quick swing of the broom, the handle broke across Dakota's back. Dakota screamed and jumped up on all fours, half asleep and confused.

"What have I told you about blocking the fan on that heater?" Mama yelled at her. "Take yourself to bed."

Dakota writhed in pain but was able to get to her bed before Mama could hit her again.

The next day was Saturday. All of the children loved Saturday's because it was the day Mama sent Dakota to Cooper's Supermarket. It was two miles to the store and Dakota picked up all the soda bottles she could find along the way. Mr. Cooper gave her four pieces of candy for every bottle. Rocky had gone to the country to stay at Aunt Hettie's for the weekend so now there would be more candy for the others.

Dakota got the grocery list and jerked the big, red wagon from the shed. "I'll fill this wagon up with bottles this time," she called to Stevie. "I haven't been to the store in almost a month. There should be plenty of bottles."

Dakota returned with a brown paper bag almost full of bubble gum and sweets. The younger children were delighted. Mama was furious.

"I told you to hurry back!" Mama glared at Dakota.

"I'm sorry, Mama. I tried but the wagon was heavy coming back home."

Mama grabbed the sack of candy from her and flung it at Stevie. "Looks like it was heavy on the way there too. Since you can't mind what I say, they can have your share. Now go bring the rest of those groceries in."

Seems like no matter what I do, I just can't please her, Dakota thought.

"I have a date tonight Dakota. I'm leaving. Put Alysa in the bed with you."

"Okay, Mama."

At three o'clock in the morning, Dakota was jerked awake. Something was wrong. Bam! Bam! Bam! Someone was banging on the window. Dakota pulled the curtain back and screamed when she saw two men staring back at her.

Alysa began to cry. Stevie and Brenden ran into the room at the same time. "What's wrong?" Brenden asked.

"Someone's out there," Dakota whispered.

BAM! BAM! BAM! "They're at the front door now," she said. Dakota jumped up and ran to check the living room door, relieved to see it was locked.

"Open up!" The man yelled. He was rattling the door knob and banging on the door. "I said open up!"

Dakota could tell from the slur in his voice that

he was drunk.

"Quick!" she told Stevie. "Check all the windows. Be sure they're locked."

She ran to check the back door, leaving Brenden and Alysa huddling on the couch. Then she picked up the phone and dialed the only number she knew.

"Mama Mary," she cried. "Come quick!" She told Mary what was happening, then hung up so Mary could call the police.

The flashing red lights on the police car were the first things Madge saw when she turned onto her street. "Oh God, what now?" she thought out loud.

She pulled into the driveway and found Dakota talking to the officer. The other children were sitting on the porch steps bundled in a blanket. She looked at Dakota in disgust. "What have you done now?" she spat.

"Nothing, Mama." Dakota's demeanor changed immediately. Whenever she was around Mama she felt like she was nothing. So she tried to look like nothing. She willed herself to be invisible. She crossed her arms and looked at the ground. She was scared to stand there. Scared to leave.

The police officer explained to Madge what was going on and admonished her for leaving the children alone. "I must have scared the men off," he said. "One of the window screens has been cut."

"I'll get the landlord to fix it," Madge replied.

"What about leaving the kids alone?" he asked.

Mama's voice became sugar sweet. "Now

honey, you know I wasn't gone that long. That big, old boss man of yours said he just had to see me tonight."

Dakota felt sick to her stomach. She turned to leave and noticed a green Buick parked in the dark, at the corner. *Mama Mary has come to check on me*, Dakota thought. Dakota didn't mention it. She knew it would make Mama mad.

Monday afternoon, Dakota came home from school to find Mama dabbing on her Jasmine perfume and knew immediately Mama was going out. Dakota took off her sneakers, plopped her books down, then went to the kitchen to make a pitcher of Kool-Aid.

"Can I have some?" Rocky had followed her into the kitchen.

"Soon as it's done," Dakota replied.

"Da-ko-ta!" Mama yelled from the bathroom. "Come here."

"Just a minute, Mama," Dakota answered. She continued to stir in the sugar.

Mama came stomping through the house. "How dare you tell me just a minute! When I call you, you come and you come now!" Mama yelled. She grabbed Dakota's ponytail and pulled her away from the table. Dakota dropped the wooden spoon. "Where's my hairbrush?" Mama demanded.

"I don't know, Mama. It should be in the bathroom."

"I know where it should be, Dakota. It's not there."

"Sometimes Alysa brushes her baby dolls' hair with it. Did you ask her?" Dakota's voice was beginning to tremble.

"Are you going to blame your stupidity on Alysa now?" Mama asked.

Dakota could see Mama was getting angrier. She began backing away until she had backed herself into a corner. "No, ma'am."

Just then Mama opened a cabinet door and took out a coffee cup. She threw the cup at Dakota's feet while Dakota jumped to keep the cup from hitting her. The cup shattered and Dakota landed on shards of glass.

Now, Dakota was sobbing.

"Oh, shut up!" Mama screamed at her. "I don't have time for this. You clean this kitchen, then you fix the kids something to eat. Then you clean the kitchen again. Then give Alysa a bath and get her ready for bed."

Mama turned and spoke to Rocky. "When she is done with all that, you put her on the back porch and lock the door. She can sleep out there tonight. Maybe by morning she will remember where my hairbrush is."

Fathers, do not exasperate your children; instead, bring them up in the training and instruction of the Lord. Ephesians 6:4

CHAPTER THREE

As soon as Mama left, Stevie got a bandage for Dakota's bleeding foot, Rocky swept up the broken pieces of glass, and Dakota stopped crying.

"Are you okay?" asked Rocky.

"I'm fine," she answered. "Just fine."

"You don't look fine," Rocky said. "You look mad."

"I'm fine, I said." Then Dakota continued her work in silence.

She cleaned and cooked and cleaned some more. She bathed the baby, put her diaper and pajamas on her, then sat on the bathroom floor thinking.

I can't sleep on the back porch, she thought. *I keep seeing those drunk men that tried to get in the house the other night. I can't.*

Rocky knocked on the bathroom door. "You done, Sis?"

"Yes," Dakota said. She opened the bathroom door. "I'm ready."

They walked to the back door together. "I hate this," Rocky said.

"I know," Dakota replied. "I do too. But it's not your fault. Mama would be mad at you if you didn't lock me out."

Rocky was three years older than Dakota. He hated the way Mama treated his sister but he had seen Mama's wrath and knew there was nothing he could do. Mostly, he stayed out of Mama's way.

Dakota stepped onto the porch and Rocky closed the door behind her. As soon as she heard the lock turn, she hit the ground running. She listened to the slap, slap sound of her bare feet hitting the asphalt for five minutes before she stopped in the darkness to catch her breath. Dakota's heart was pounding so hard, she could feel it moving her sweatshirt. Her throat hurt and for a split second she thought about going back home.

Well, you've done it now, she thought. *You've run away. Now what?*

The sound of an animal scurrying in the bushes scared her on. She ran again not stopping until she reached Cooper's Supermarket. The store was closed but the laundry mat next door was open. Dakota went inside. The place was empty. She sneezed when the strong smell of powdered detergent hit her nostrils. "Owie," she complained. Her mouth was dry, her breathing labored.

She began sticking two fingers into the coin return slot on each of the washers and dryers. It was something she did every Saturday when she did the grocery shopping. No money. Then she remembered the snack machine. Jackpot! Fifteen cents.

Clutching the money tightly, Dakota ran to the phone booth just outside the laundry mat. The light was burned out inside the booth but the lights on the front of the building were enough to see the numbers on the phone. She deposited ten cents. Her fingers were shaking as she dialed the number - partly because it was getting cold, partly because she was scared. The phone rang four times. No answer. Three more times. Dakota was getting worried.

Finally, Mary answered. "Hello?" she said sleepily.

"Mama Mary! I was getting afraid you wouldn't be home," Dakota said matter-of-factly.

"I'm home, honey. What's wrong?"

"I ran away."

"What?" Mary was wide awake now.

"I ran away," Dakota repeated.

"Where are you?" Mary asked.

"I'm at the phone booth near Cooper's on Boulder Avenue," she replied.

"Stay right where you are," Mary said. "Don't go anywhere else."

"I won't," Dakota promised.

Dakota waited in the cold night air for Mama Mary to come get her. It seemed like a long time before she saw headlights approaching.

Finally, she thought.

The car pulled up right next to the phone booth. It was not Mary. It was a yellow cab. Dakota shrank back into the booth trying to hide.

"Hey! You, in there!" the driver yelled. "Your name Dakota?"

"Y..yes," she stammered.

"A lady named Mary asked me to pick you up and bring you to her house. That okay with you?"

Dakota breathed a sigh of relief and climbed into the taxi.

The car was warm and the quiet hum of the motor put Dakota to sleep. When they pulled into the driveway, Mary was on the porch waiting.

"Hey, kid." The driver woke her. "We're here."

"I'll get you some money," Dakota told him.

After paying the fare, Dakota and Mary went inside to the bright kitchen and mugs filled with hot chocolate.

Finally, when Dakota began talking it was as though a dam had burst. She told Mary everything - how Mama had beat her, kicked her, spit on her, cursed her and sometimes made her go hungry. She told why her grades weren't always good and why she fell asleep in class. She told why she tried to steal makeup and confessed she had stolen food.

Mary cried quietly as she listened to Dakota. She had loved this child since birth. How could anyone treat their own child this way?

Ding-dong. The doorbell chime was extra loud in the quiet of the night. Dakota stiffened, her eyes reflecting the fear that gripped her. Mary placed her hand on Dakota's shoulder.

"You stay here," she said. "I'll see who it is."

Mary expected to find Madge at the front door. It was a policeman.

Dakota leaned toward the archway that led to the front room and strained to hear what was being said. She couldn't quite make it out.

Mama Mary had been gone for five minutes when she came back to the kitchen table. She took Dakota's hand and squeezed it.

"I'm sorry, honey," she said softly. "There's a policeman here. He's come to take you back home."

Hot tears began to roll down Dakota's cheeks.

"I don't have any say in the matter," Mary told her. "The police say you are her child and it is not against the law to discipline your own child."

"Maybe Big Daddy could talk to him." Dakota took in a ragged breath.

"Big Daddy had to drive a rig to North Carolina and he won't be home tonight, honey."

"Ma'am," the policeman called.

"We'll be right there," Mary called back.

Mary and Dakota walked to the living room. The policeman was the same one that picked Dakota up for shoplifting.

"You!" he said. "Well, you're just a regular little troublemaker now ain't you?"

Dakota dropped her chin to her chest. Mary pulled her close.

"That's not necessary," Mary scolded him. Then she placed her fingers under Dakota's chin and lifted her head. She looked into the girls tear-filled eyes. "You are someone special," she told her. "Square your shoulders and walk tall with your head held high. You have nothing to be ashamed of. Don't be hanging your head like that and don't be scared. God's angels will be watching over you."

"Let's go," the officer said.

Dakota huddled in the corner of the back seat but she didn't sleep this time. This time she didn't feel safe.

Mama was waiting outside when they arrived. It was the middle of the night and as soon as the policeman left, Mama led Dakota to the shed behind the house. Dakota saw the belt hanging on a nail inside the door and knew what was coming.

With every lash of the belt, Mama's tongue lashed her too.

"You will listen to me," Mama yelled, and brought the leather strap down on her hard. Dakota stiffened. The tears began. "You will mind me." She brought it down even harder. "You will not disobey." On and on it went. When mama was done, she left Dakota alone in the dark shed, and bolted the door shut.

The next morning, Stevie unlocked the shed

door and Dakota went inside to get ready for school. As Dakota cooked some Cream of Wheat for breakfast, Mama noticed the welts she had left on Dakota's legs.

"Go change your clothes, Dakota."

"I already did, Mama."

Mama raised her voice. "I said go change your clothes," she barked. "This time put on long pants."

After Dakota ran away, Mama tightened the reins on her even more. No more walking to school or Cooper's Market alone. Now she had to have Stevie or Brenden with her. Mama knew she wouldn't run off and leave them.

Saturday morning, Mama had to see the landlord and left all five kids at home. Dakota was instructed to clean the house and began cleaning as soon as Mama left. The last thing on her list was wax the floors. She put Alysa down for her nap and told Stevie and Brenden to play outside until the floor dried. The two small boys began their favorite game of *chase*. Ignoring what Dakota told them, they began chasing each other across the wet floor.

"You can't catch me!" Stevie said.

Brenden giggled and ran after him. Both of them left tracks in the wet wax.

"I'm going to break your neck!" Dakota yelled at them. Stevie stuck his thumbs in his ears and wiggled his fingers. He stuck his tongue out at Dakota and began to sing, *"Na-na-na-na-na-na!"*

Dakota set the can of wax on the table and took off after him. Stevie ran out the front door, around the house and in the back door, with Dakota on his heels. As soon as he was in the house he slammed the back door shut just as Dakota started in. The lock on the door was set to automatically lock when the door was closed. With the door closing fast and Dakota running toward it she reached up to stop it. The door locked and her hand went through the glass!

Cast all your anxiety on Him because He cares for you. 1 Peter 5:7

CHAPTER FOUR

For a few seconds there was total silence. Stevie and Brenden stared at Dakota. Dakota stared at her arm as it was quickly covered in blood. Stevie thought Dakota might faint. He opened the door, grabbed her other arm, and led her to the couch. He pulled a towel from the laundry basket and wrapped it around her injured arm.

Dakota couldn't help but think about how mad Mama was going to be. Blood had dripped to the floor from the back door to the living room.

"I'll be alright", she said. "Just get me a band-aid."

"I'm not a doctor," Stevie told her, "But even I know this is going to need more than a band-aid. Brenden, you stay right here. I'll go to Mrs. Phillips for help." Stevie got just past the front steps when he saw Mama's old Ford pull into the driveway.

Dakota was more worried about Mama than her arm and when she looked up to see Madge walk in the front door she turned even paler. "Mama, I am so sorry. It was an accident. I'll clean up the mess."

Madge looked at Dakota's arm and told her to get in the car just as Rocky walked in. "Where have you been?" Mama asked him.

"Next door," he replied. "What happened to Dakota?"

"Never mind that now," Mama told him. "I'm taking her to the emergency room. You watch the kids."

Dakota watched the nurse pull the curtain and Mama leave the room.

"You don't have to leave," the nurse told Madge.

"I just need to use the phone," Madge replied.

Dakota tried her best to be brave. Closing her eyes tight, she turned her head away from the doctor as he stitched up her arm.

"There are two places I'll have to sew," he said. "One of those places will have to be stitched on the inside first, then on the outside.

Dakota was feeling queasy. "Oh, please don't tell me," she begged. "Just do it."

"Here comes the stick," the doctor said.

She cringed and stiffened as he gave her several small shots to deaden the area around the largest cut.

Dakota had figured out two ways to escape pain. Sometimes she would daydream. Sometimes she would sleep. So while the doctor sewed her arm, she fell fast asleep.

The curtain was pulled open and the nurse told the doctor someone named Mary would be there soon to pick Dakota up. Mama had left. She didn't even say goodbye.

Dakota awoke as Mary laid her on the back seat of the Buick. Her arm was bandaged from her elbow to her wrist and now it began to throb.

"Go back to sleep," Mary said. "We'll be home soon."

Dakota enjoyed another three weeks of staying with Mama Mary. Mrs. Cleveland adjusted Dakota's studies since she couldn't use her right hand. The doctor said there was nerve damage and that there would be an area on her arm that would be numb for the rest of her life. Dakota didn't mind. It was just one less place to feel pain.

Mary took Dakota shopping for some new clothes, took her to church, and took her to visit Mary's niece, Barb. The time flew by. All too soon she was back at home.

The days at home passed by slowly. Day after day of school, watching the younger children and cooking and cleaning had Dakota daydreaming a lot. She did her best to stay out of Mama's way and to stay out of trouble. But Dakota knew the peace she now enjoyed would not last.

Colder weather was fast approaching and Saturday morning the children awoke to a rare treat.

There was a light blanket of snow on the ground. One by one, there came a screech of joy. The noise woke Mama and put her in a bad mood.

"Shhh," Dakota admonished. "Not so loud. Mama's sleeping."

"Too late for that," Mama said, as she entered the living room. "Why do ya'll have to be so loud? Go wake Rocky up, Dakota. Since today is your birthday your Granny wants us to drive down to the country. We'll probably spend the night, so throw some of the kids' clothes in a bag."

Dakota was excited. She had forgotten it was her birthday. She loved snow and she loved going to Granny's house.

Everyone was piling into the car when Dakota remembered to check the mail. She ran back to the car excitedly ripping open the envelope addressed to her. She knew it was a birthday card from Mama Mary. As she pulled the card from the envelope a twenty dollar bill fell to the ground.

Mama reached down and scooped up the money. "I'll just hold on to this for you," she said. Dakota knew she would never get it back but decided to not let it ruin her birthday. Turning twelve was supposed to be a big deal.

It would take an hour and a half to get to Granny's house, so Dakota crawled into the back seat with Stevie and Brenden and quickly got them interested in the coloring books she brought along. Then she settled back for some serious daydreaming.

"Uncle Ken is here!" Rocky announced as they pulled into Granny's dirt driveway. Everyone clamored out of the car.

Dakota was the first one to reach uncle Ken. "Well if it ain't my favorite tomboy," he drawled. "Happy Birthday, Kiddo." He returned her bear hug. Ken pulled a slingshot from his back pocket and shoved it at Dakota. "Made it myself," he said. "Now you be careful with it."

Mama walked by them and confiscated the slingshot before Dakota even touched it. "I'll make sure of that, brother," Mama said, and kept walking.

"Aw, Madge, come on. She's twelve now."

Madge just ignored him and entered the house letting the screen door slam behind her.

"Thanks anyway, Uncle Ken," Dakota told him. She looked around breathing in the country air. Next to Mary's, this was the next best place to be.

Granny's house was old and had never seen paint. It was surrounded by big oaks and walnut trees. The yard was mostly dirt and the nearest neighbor was over a mile away. In the summer, the children would sleep on a pallet on the floor. Granny would place a fan at the door to bring in cooler air and Dakota loved to sleep there.

Tonight though, she would have a pallet near the woodstove. The smoke of the hickory burning in that stove was part of the country air she breathed in now.

"Mmmmm," said Dakota. "That smells so good."

"You just think that smells good," Uncle Ken told her. "Wait 'til you get inside."

Meals at Granny's house had been the same for years. Granny raised nine children on very little money. So she came up with ways to feed them all without much complaint. There were three meals a day - breakfast, dinner, supper.

Breakfast was always Granny's tender, flaky biscuits and whatever you could find to go on them - homemade peach preserves, milk gravy, or real butter with cane syrup. Supper was always cornbread and milk. Sometimes sweet milk; sometimes buttermilk. Dinner was the mid-day meal and the biggest. Usually ham or fried chicken or fish Grandpa and Granny caught. Sometimes there was turtle stew with never-ending vegetables from Granny's garden. Even in winter, she had jars and jars of canned goods and if you were lucky there were biscuits left over from breakfast.

Dakota ran up the steps and into the rickety house. "Ummm, fried chicken," she exclaimed. She went to the kitchen to find the tiny wrinkled woman she loved so much. Dakota was only twelve but already she was taller than Granny. She put her arms around the woman's frail frame and hugged. "I've missed you, Granny," she said.

"I've missed you too, child. Come look."

Granny led Dakota to the side pantry next to the back door. She opened a cabinet and Dakota let out a whoop! Sitting there on an antique plate was a five-layer cake with homemade chocolate icing between each layer.

Dakota picked up a tiny piece of the hardened icing and popped it into her mouth. "You've outdone yourself this time, Granny," she purred. "You have to teach me how to make that icing."

Granny smiled. She had many grandchildren but this one made her feel special. "Happy Birthday, Dakota."

After dinner, Rocky rode home with Uncle Ken. Granny made the youngest children take a nap so she and Mama could lay down to rest too.

Dakota slipped outside. The snowfall from the night before left only a dusting here and there and it was already beginning to melt. Dakota decided to explore and headed for the White Horse Canyons. The White Horse Canyons weren't canyons at all. They were a maze of deep gullies made of red clay and rock. Legend has it that Cherokee natives chased and trapped wild horses there and Dakota loved to look for arrowheads in the shallow caves. She broke a length of reed cane as she began her adventure and poked the stick into the holes in the side of the red slopes. As she wandered, she remembered the summer she spent there and how it had rained every day. The deep sides of the gullies had been wet and sticky, and she slid down them time after time on a broken-down cardboard box. What fun that summer had been. The more her mind wandered, the deeper into the maze she went, until at long last Dakota realized she was lost!

Supper time came and Ken and Rocky returned to Granny's house. Then, Grandpa came in from laying brick all day. Grandpa was a handsome, hazel-eyed, robust man.

"I'm starving," he said. "When is supper?" he asked Granny.

"Just waiting for Dakota to come in," she replied.

"Well where is she?" Grandpa asked. "I didn't see her when I came up the driveway. She should have come running."

"Oh, Lord!" Granny exclaimed. "You know how she loves the canyons. I'll bet that's where she is."

"She better not be," Mama said. "I've told her not to go in there."

Granny began to wring her hands. "Come to think of it, I haven't seen her all afternoon."

Uncle Ken gave Granny's shoulder a squeeze. "Now don't you go getting upset," he told her. "She probably just lost track of time. If she is in the canyons, I'll teach her a lesson she won't soon forget." He went looking and found Dakota but he didn't let her see him. The girl didn't know it but Uncle Ken could holler exactly like a bobcat, and that is what he did.

"Yeeeoww!"

Dakota froze. *What on earth was that?* she wondered. She pulled her pink jacket tightly around her.

"Yeeeoww!"

This time it was even louder. At first Dakota thought it was a woman screaming. Now she wasn't sure. Whatever it was, Dakota was not sticking around to meet it. Her long legs carried her like the wind twisting and turning back through the maze to where the old house stood in the clearing. Dakota ran into the house breathing hard and gasping for air.

"Oh, Dakota," Granny said. "You had us so worried."

Mama walked over to Dakota and pulled her close as though to hug her. "I'll take care of you when we get home," she murmured. "How dare you embarrass me like this."

Dakota hung her head. "I'm sorry Granny. It won't happen again."

Do not be anxious about anything, but in every situation, by prayer and petition, with thanksgiving, present your requests to God. Philippians 4:6

CHAPTER FIVE

Time passed and the holiday season came. Mama didn't know and Dakota dared not tell her Mama Mary had volunteered to host the Christmas party for Mrs. Cleveland's class. The teacher asked Dakota to pass around the goodies. Dakota was excited. After the class party, Mary and Dakota sat down to visit for a few minutes.

"I'm so happy to see you, Mama Mary. Thank you for the party."

"I'm happy to see you too, sweetie. I've missed hearing from you."

Dakota looked down at her feet. "I'm not going to live with her forever, you know."

"What? Where did that come from?"

"I hate living with Mama. I'm tired of how she treats me. I want to come live with you." Dakota squirmed in her seat and then looked Mary square in the eye. "If I keep running away and come to your house...."

Mary interrupted Dakota. "If you keep running to my house," she said, "the police will keep taking you back to her. All that will do is make her even more mad at you."

"You don't want me," Dakota said matter-of-factly.

"That's not true, Dakota. I ask God to watch over you and keep you safe every night and every morning. I would give up my life for you. Big Daddy and I love you more than anyone in the world. But if your Mama won't let you live with us, there's nothing we can do. Do you remember when you prayed, Dakota? Asking God to forgive you for all you do wrong?"

"Yes Ma'am," she answered.

"He not only forgives you, but promised He would help you and have His angels watch over you. You have to trust Him."

Dakota's eyes filled with tears. She wiped at them and hugged Mary tightly. Then she ran out of the classroom and walked home.

Christmas morning all of the children had two packages under the tree. The younger boys had cowboy hats and guns with holsters. Alysa had a doll and cradle. Rocky got exactly what he wanted - new pants and a sweater. Dakota opened the boxes with her name - new gloves and school supplies.

"What was that noise?" asked Mama. Dakota looked out the window. First she gasped then she squealed. There on the front porch was a large box of brightly colored packages. Dakota could see the children's names on them. Sitting beside the box was a pink 26" bicycle with a gift card hanging from the handlebar.

Dakota ran out the front door with Mama at her heels. When Dakota saw her name on the card, she sat on the bike.

"Get off the bicycle, Dakota," Mama told her.

"But Mama it's mine. The card has my name on it."

Mama slapped her across the face hard. "I said get off of it." Mama grabbed Dakota by the arm and jerked her off the bike. She pushed her back into the house and locked the door.

A while later Dakota could hear Mama on the phone. "Let me speak to Mary." There was a moment of silence. Then, "Come get this stuff off of my porch."

Dakota thought if she lived to be a hundred she would never understand her Mama.

Spring came. Dakota and the other children were happy to go outside to play. A girl they did not recognize walked by the house. Dakota watched the girl but was too shy to speak so the girl spoke to her.

"Hello," she said. "My name is Valerie. I just moved here. Two streets over. What's your name?"

"Dakota."

"That's an interesting name. Never heard it before. How old are you?"

"Twelve."

"Me too. Just turned twelve, actually."

Dakota studied the girl as she rambled on and on. She was about the same height as Dakota but a little chubby. Her strawberry-blond hair was short and her violet eyes danced as she talked.

"So, would you like to come over to my house?" Valerie asked her.

"Oh. Maybe some other time," Dakota replied. "I have to baby-sit right now."

Dakota knew the polite thing to do was to invite Valerie to stay for awhile but she never invited anyone because of Mama.

However, Valerie joined Mrs. Cleveland's class and the girls became friends over time. She took an afternoon walk almost every day and usually stopped to chat with Dakota. Once, she asked Dakota to walk with her.

Mama overheard and to Dakota's surprise told her she could go. "Just be back by six," Mama said.

The girls walked, talked, and giggled. Soon they were walking to school together with Stevie and Brenden tagging along. To Dakota's surprise, she found she had a friend.

Walking home from school, Dakota saw the old Ford coming toward them. "Here comes my Mama", she said.

The car stopped. "Get in the car," Mama said.

Can we give Valerie a ride?" Dakota asked.

"No," Mama replied.

"Sorry, Val. Got to go."

As Mama drove away, she spoke to Dakota. "I don't want you hanging around that girl anymore," she said.

"But, Mama, she's my friend."

Mama slapped her across the mouth. "Don't back talk me."

That night, Dakota sneaked out.

"But I am telling you she is not here," Mary told the Officer.

"Mind if I look around?" he asked.

Mary opened the door wide and invited him in. It was after midnight and Dakota was missing. The policeman looked at Mary closely.

"When she ran away the last time, she came here. Is that right?"

"Yes," Mary answered. "But I have not seen her in several weeks. She hasn't called either." Mary followed him down the hall. "You can look around here all you want," she told him, "but I am going to get in my car and look for her myself."

"That won't be necessary," the officer replied. "We'll find her."

Together they walked back to the front door.

"Wait!" Mary reached out and touched his arm. "Please call me when you find her."

Mary reached for a pencil and paper to write down her phone number. "I love that little girl," she said as she shoved the paper into his hand. "I don't get along with her mother, but I love her. Please let me know that she's okay."

"Alright," the officer said. "Tell me, why does she keep running away?"

"Her mother treats her badly," Mary told him. "The things I could tell you," she said, shaking her head.

"Any idea where she might be?" he asked.

"No", Mary replied. "She has always come to me when things got bad. I'm really worried this time."

No one knew where Dakota was because Dakota had not told anyone. She decided this time she was not going back. This time she planned ahead. For several days, Dakota sneaked things into the shed. She brought an empty cardboard box from Cooper's store and took a paper bag from the kitchen. She filled them with clothes, a jar of peanut butter, saltine crackers, and some canned pork and beans. Every day, Dakota walked through the house looking to see if there was anything else she wanted to take with her. The nights were chilly, so she packed a small blanket. She knew she would miss her brothers and sister, so she found a snapshot of all the children together. Then she put the Bible Mama Mary had given her in the box.

For several weeks, Dakota turned in as many bottles as she could find to Mr. Cooper. She asked him to give her the nickel deposit on them instead of the candy he had been giving. Now, she had several dollars in a mason jar at the bottom of the box.

She was spending the first night on her own in Valerie's garage.

"Daddy is gone to Georgia to help my Grandma with moving," Valerie said. "Mom's cooking supper. She will never know you're here."

It was just about bedtime when Valerie sneaked a paper plate loaded with corned beef and cabbage into the garage. "How long you going to stay?" she asked Dakota.

"I think I should keep moving," the girl replied. "They will probably be looking here soon. I'll leave when I wake up." Dakota wolfed down her food.

"Okay," Valerie said. She handed Dakota a piece of paper. "Here is our phone number. You call if you need me. Mom said I could walk to the park Saturday. The big park near town. Why don't you meet me there?"

"What time?" Dakota asked.

"Around lunch time. I'll bring you something to eat."

"Okay." The girls hugged and Dakota slept.

The next morning, Dakota slipped outside to the hosepipe for a drink of water and splashed some on her face. She then headed to the nearest service station where there was a public restroom. She took a wash cloth from her belongings to give herself a sponge bath. Hiding her box, she went inside the station to buy a small pack of donuts and a soda for breakfast.

Dakota remembered what Valerie said about the park. Today was Friday, so Valerie wouldn't be there until tomorrow but the park seemed like a good idea. She could blend in with the other kids there. She just had to find a hiding place for her belongings.

Once she arrived at the park, she noticed a culvert near a stream. She put her box and bag inside the culvert then went to look around. It was early and the park was empty. She walked across the baseball field and down the steps into the cement block dugout. *Hmmm,* she thought, *This would be the perfect place to stay tonight.*

Dakota ran back to the culvert to retrieve her goods and placed them under the wooden bench inside the dugout. Younger children came and went throughout the day. Dakota passed the time with some of them. She snacked on peanut butter and crackers and at supper time walked two blocks to get a burger. She knew her money would run out eventually. She decided she would have to start looking for bottles to redeem soon. She didn't know what she was going to do if she couldn't buy food. She just knew that anything was better than going home to Mama.

Dear children, let us not love with words or speech but with actions and in truth. 1 John 3:18

CHAPTER SIX

Good to her word, Valerie showed up on Saturday right at lunch time. She handed Dakota a sandwich wrapped in waxed paper. "Guess what," she said. "Robin is having a pajama party tonight. I've been invited and she said I could bring a friend."

"Who's Robin?" Dakota asked.

"The girl you saw at my house the other day, silly. Remember I told you to hide because my cousin was coming up the walk?"

"Yeah. I remember now."

"Well, her mother is going to take all of us girls swimming at the Y. Then we are going to her house for a weenie and marshmallow roast. Mmmm...s'mores."

"Sounds good," Dakota replied.

"You want to go with me?"

"I'd better not," Dakota told her. "What if they know I ran away?"

"I haven't told anyone. How will they know?"

"Besides. I don't have pajamas or a swimsuit."

"You can use some of my cousins' stuff. She is about the same size as you and it is a chance for you to get some hot food." Valerie put her hands under her chin in a begging gesture. "Please? Please go with me?"

"Oh, alright. It's not like I have anything else to do."

"Okay, I'm riding my bike to Robin's. Meet me at the corner of Willow Road at six o'clock. Wait near the bus stop, then we will go to Robin's together."

Dakota gave her a *thumbs up* and munched on the tuna salad sandwich her friend had brought her.

After Valerie left, Dakota sat on the swings for a long time thinking. She wasn't as scared as when she first ran away but she was beginning to get lonely. She began to think about Mama Mary. She started walking and walked until she came to a phone booth. She stepped inside and dropped a dime into the slot and dialed the number.

"Hello?"

Dakota hesitated. "I just wanted to let you know I am alright, Mama Mary." Hot tears ran down her cheeks.

"Dakota! Where are you, honey?"

Dakota hung up the phone. *If Mama Mary doesn't know where I am*, she thought, *she can't get into trouble.*

The girls met at six o'clock that evening. Valerie got off her bike and the two walked side-by-side to Robin's house.

"Have you walked by my house lately?" Dakota asked.

"Yes, I did today."

"Did you see any of my brothers? Or my sister?"

"Yep. As a matter-of-fact, I saw Stevie. He waved at me."

"I miss him," Dakota whined. "I miss them all. Except Mama."

"Here's where Robin lives," Valerie interrupted.

Dakota could hear the squeals and laughter coming from inside the brick house. The door flew open and three teenagers came bounding down the steps. They were a couple of years older than Dakota and Valerie.

"Hi, Robin," Valerie said.

"Hey, little cousin," Robin replied.

"Robin, this is my friend, Dakota."

"Hey! Now ya'll get in the car. We're going swimming. Here is the stuff you wanted to borrow." Robin shoved a small bag toward Dakota.

Robin's mother drove them to the YMCA. Everyone clamored from the car and headed for the door.

One of the girls was named Margie. She had bushy red hair and lots of freckles.

Dakota thought she was pretty and kept staring

at her.

It caught Margie's attention and she stared back. A look of recognition came across Margie's face. "Hey! You're that girl everybody has been looking for!"

Dakota dropped her bag and ran until she could run no more. Her sides ached and it was hard to catch her breath. *I should have known better,* she thought. *I should have stayed at the park. But Valerie won't tell where I'm staying. I know she won't.* Dakota still had a long way to go to get back to the park. She decided to stay on the side roads as much as possible. The main road was a busy one and sure to have police patrolling it. When she did have to get on the main road, she ran to get to the next back road quickly. Nightfall was coming and Dakota wished she were already at the dugout. Finally she decided to walk the rest of the way on the main road. She soon heard footsteps on the sidewalk behind her and turned to see who it was.

A young man was a few yards back. He was grungy and needed a shave. Dakota had seen the look in his eyes before and wondered if he was drunk. She decided to cross the road and as she did, he crossed too.

"Oh, brother!" Dakota said out loud. She sped her pace and from the sound of his footsteps she knew he had too. Dakota began running as fast as her tired legs would carry her. She crossed the road again and so did he. Dakota was scared now.

Coming to an intersection she turned right and continued to run uphill toward a small store. She looked over her shoulder to see if the man was still chasing her when...*bam!* She ran smack into something and bounced backward. Dakota turned her head to see what she had hit. Standing before her was the tallest, largest man she had ever seen and he was a cop!

The officer looked down at Dakota. He pushed his round hat back, placed his hands on his hips and frowned.

"Your name Dakota?" he asked.

"Yes, sir," Dakota replied weakly, panting.

The officer looked over her head. "How long has he been chasing you?"

Dakota was desperately trying to catch her breath. "Since the Sears building," she told him.

He reached over and opened the back door of the patrol car. "Get in!" he barked.

Dakota did as she was told, but then pleaded with him, "Please, please, sir. Don't take me back home."

"I'm not," he said, as he slammed the door.

He slid into the front seat and began talking into a microphone.

Dakota's thoughts ran wildly through her mind. *How did he know it was me? How did he know that man was chasing me? Why isn't he taking me home?*

She voiced these questions and the officer

replied, "We've been looking all over town for you," he said and added, "I watched that man cross the street chasing you. Do you know him?"

"No, Sir." Dakota fidgeted with her ponytail. "Where are you taking me? Can I go to Mama Mary's?"

"No," the officer said.

"But if I'm not going home and I can't go to Mama Mary's, then where are we going?"

The officer put the car in gear. "To the Children's Center."

"What is the Children's Center?" she asked.

"It's a place we take kids when they have no place else to go."

"But I do have a place," Dakota insisted. "I can go to Mama Mary's. I can tell you how to get there."

"Sorry, kiddo," the officer replied. "Your Mama said she didn't care where we took you as long as we didn't take you there."

Dakota began to cry quietly. All she wanted was to be with someone who loved her. The people at the Children's Center didn't even know her.

The car pulled up in front of a long brick building and stopped. Dakota had seen it before but didn't know what is was. The front door opened and a middle aged woman stepped out. She wore a blue matronly dress and her brown hair was pulled into a knot at the back of her head. Square glasses sat on the end of her nose and she squinted as she looked Dakota over.

"Well, come in, come in," she said. She stepped back to allow Dakota and the officer to go inside.

Standing in the foyer, Dakota could see a formal room to the right with fancy furniture that looked like it had never been sat on. To the left was a den where three children sat watching a nature program on the television set.

"My name is Miss Geneva," the woman said.

The policeman introduced Dakota and turned to tell her she would be staying with Miss Geneva for a while, and he left.

Dakota felt she was in the twilight zone. *How could he just dump her off on someone she didn't even know?* she thought.

"Well, Dakota, you don't have any belongings with you, do you?"

"No, ma'am." Dakota suddenly felt vulnerable.

"Okay, come with me. We'll see what we can find for you to sleep in, and Monday we'll go shopping." Miss Geneva produced a pair of pink pajamas, some underwear, and a pair of socks from a closet in the hallway. She led the girl to a room at the end of the building. The room was surprisingly large. Three beds lined one wall. Three dressers with mirrors lined the opposite wall. The first bed had a bedspread and pillow on it. The other two had folded bed linens laying on the striped mattresses.

"This bed belongs to Tonya," Miss Geneva said. "She's visiting her father this weekend. You'll meet her Sunday night. You may choose one of the other beds and you're responsible for making your bed every day."

Dakota went to the back of the room and sat down on the last bed.

Miss Geneva went to the last dresser, pulled open the top drawer, and retrieved a plastic bag. "This is yours. Use it please. The bathroom is just across the hall. I'll be back in a little while."

Dakota dumped the bag onto the mattress. There was a wash cloth and towel, a brush, a toothbrush, toothpaste, soap, shampoo and a small New Testament Bible. The Bible reminded her of Mama Mary and she began to cry again. After her shower, Dakota felt better and went about putting the bed linens on her bed.

Miss Geneva came into the room. "There is a plastic box under your bed," she said. That is where you put your dirty clothes. You will be washing them every Saturday. I'll wash these tonight," she said as she picked up Dakota's clothes from the dresser top. "You will need something clean for tomorrow."

Dakota finished the bed and stood pulling at her wet hair.

"What have you eaten today?" Miss Geneva asked her.

"Tuna fish sandwich."

"Come with me." She led Dakota down the hall to a dining room filled with long tables. "Sit here," she said.

She stepped into the kitchen. Dakota could see

her through a large opening in the wall and watched her pull a plate of fried chicken from the refrigerator. "How's this?" she asked, calling back.

"Fine", Dakota said. "I love cold chicken."

"Good." Miss Geneva put the chicken and a glass of milk in front of her. "Eat what you want and off to bed with you."

Dakota was exhausted. She fell into bed and was asleep in no time. Sleep was her escape.

The king will reply, "Truly I tell you, whatever you did for one of the least of these brothers and sisters of mine, you did for me." Matthew 25:40

CHAPTER SEVEN

The next day was Sunday. Dakota didn't have church clothes, so Miss Geneva said she would stay with her while the other children went to church. Dakota could hear the church bus horn honking impatiently. She found her clothes folded neatly on the dresser and changed quickly. Quietly, she made her bed and sat on it. Dakota didn't know what she was supposed to do now. She was in a strange place. She longed for Mama Mary. The times she had gone to church on Sunday it had been Mama Mary who had taken her and she wished she was there now.

There was a knock at the open door. Miss Geneva stuck her head in and smiled at Dakota.

"Time for breakfast," she sang.

Dakota followed her to the dining room. Miss Geneva talked to her as she ate her pancakes and bacon. "These first few days will be a time of adjustment for you," Miss Geneva said. "You will soon learn where everything is. You will learn our schedule and routine and eventually you will learn the names of all the children."

"How many children are there?" Dakota asked.

"Well, right now there are eleven. Sometimes we have more, sometimes less. There's another lady who helps out from time to time - her name is Mrs. Batson. She's awfully nice. You will meet her soon."

Dakota squirmed around on the metal chair. "How long will I have to stay here," she asked.

Miss Geneva sat down across from Dakota and studied her face. "That depends on a lot of things," she told her. "Mostly it depends on you. Do you think you could be happy here?"

Dakota shrugged her shoulders. "I don't know," she replied. "You see, there is this person named Mama Mary. She's the only one that ever cared about me. I love her. She loves me. Why can't I go to her house?"

"Who is Mama Mary?" asked the woman.

"I've known her all my life. Her and my mother were best friends. She was my baby-sitter when I was little. But her and Mama aren't friends anymore."

"Why are you *not* staying with your mother?" Miss Geneva inquired.

Dakota laid the fork down on the plate. She stared at the table and didn't answer. She couldn't answer. She was too scared. If Mama found out, she would hurt her again, and Dakota didn't trust anyone.

Miss Geneva didn't push her for an answer. She showed Dakota where to scrape her plate and took her on a tour of the house and grounds. The back yard looked like a park with its playground and benches. The south wing of the building was for girls. The north wing housed the boys. The dining room divided the two.

Dakota's favorite part was the basement. This was shared by all. It was a recreational room with ping-pong tables, shelves with books, easy chairs and tables for playing board games.

"You may come to the basement after homework hour in the evening and anytime during the weekend except for meals or church time," Miss Geneva told her.

She left her in the basement to explore the books until the dinner bell rang.

That evening, Tonya - Dakota's roommate - returned from visiting her father. Dakota was surprised when she saw her. Tonya looked like a grownup! The girl was tall and beautiful.

"Hi," Tonya said.

Dakota had just come from the showers and was getting ready for bed.

"Hi," she said timidly.

"My name is Tonya. Who are you?"

"Dakota."

"Haven't seen you before, Dakota. When did you get here?"

"Yesterday."

"Ah," said Tonya. "A brand newbie! Well, don't you worry about a thing! If you have any questions, just ask me." Tonya unpacked a small suitcase as she talked. Her shoulder-length blond hair swayed with every word. Dakota couldn't help but notice her blue eye shadow was exactly the color of her eyes.

"How old are you?" asked Dakota.

"I'll be eighteen in a couple of months," the girl replied.

"I thought this place was just for kids."

"It is," Tonya said. "I'll be leaving on my birthday."

"Why don't you stay with your father?" Dakota asked.

"Because I just met him a few months ago. We're getting to know each other and he's helping me find a new place to live."

"Oh," Dakota replied. "So, why don't you live with your mother?"

"My mother died five years ago. I must have been about your age. That's when I came here." Tonya paused. "Dakota, when I said you could ask questions, I meant about the Children's Center, not about me!"

"Sorry," Dakota told her.

Tonya smiled at her and winked. "I think you and I will be good friends."

Dakota slept late on Monday morning. When she awoke, Miss Geneva took her shopping for several outfits and later for transferring to a new school. Dakota was not happy. "But I'll miss everyone at my school," she whined. My friend and my brothers, and Mrs. Cleveland."

"This is a fresh new start for you, Dakota," Miss Geneva told her. "Besides, all the children at the Center go to the schools in this school district."

"When can I see Mama Mary?" demanded Dakota.

"We'll have to have a talk with your case worker," she said. "I can't promise anything until we have a meeting with her."

The next morning Tonya shook Dakota awake. "Rise and shine sleepy-head."

Dakota was beginning to catch on to the routine of getting dressed, making the bed, and eating breakfast. By the time the children were called to leave for school she was ready. She was glad she had new clothes. Heading for the door, she noticed the children were lining up in the hallway. Miss Geneva sat at a small table near the door. "What's all this?" Dakota asked Tonya.

"Every morning on our way to school we pick up our daily allowance."

"What's a daily allowance?"

"The little kids ride the school bus so they just get lunch money. Big kids like you and me get lunch money and bus fare to and from downtown because that is where our school is.

Dakota watched as the children stopped to pick

up the tiny yellow envelopes. She whispered to Tonya, "Do I have to buy lunch or can I just keep the money?"

"It's your money but you better use the bus fare."

"I've never been on a city bus," Dakota told her.

"First time for everything," Tonya said. "Just stick with me."

The next few weeks Dakota continued to settle into her new life adjusting to school and the Center. Then came the day Tonya had to leave. Dakota found herself crying. She sat on her bed watching Tonya pack the last of her things. "Do you have to go?" she asked Tonya.

"Yes, rules are rules," Tonya reminded her. "The rules say I can stay until I turn eighteen. Look on the bright side...you'll have the room all to yourself." Tonya sat down beside Dakota and put her arm around her. "That was a great party today. Miss Geneva said you helped bake the cake. That was my favorite part. Thank you."

"You're welcome. But I still don't want you to go."

"You'll be fine and I'll call you." Tonya kissed the top of Dakota's head, grabbed her bag, and left the room.

Dakota spent the rest of the day in her room alone. Now she missed Mama Mary more than ever and couldn't understand why she couldn't see her. Her case worker wouldn't even let her talk to her on the phone. Dakota was tired of waiting and decided to do something about it. That night, she stuffed as much of her personal belongings as she could into her book bag. *I'll skip school tomorrow,* she thought. *I'll go back to the dugout at the park. I was safe there. Then I can call Mama Mary.*

She could not believe her eyes when she arrived at the dugout. The box of her old belongings was still there pushed far back under the bench. She was glad. It was a cool night and she needed the small blanket. She drifted off to sleep with thoughts of visiting Valerie tomorrow.

Dakota sat straight up. Someone was shaking her awake. She must have slept late because the sun was high and she heard the sounds of toddlers on the playground.

There were three of them - teenage boys. Dakota's eyes darted back and forth as she looked at them sizing them up. "What do you want?" she asked.

The one that shook her awake spoke first. "Aw don't be that way, cutie. We just wanted to say, hi."

"What's your name, sweet stuff?" asked the second boy.

Dakota didn't answer. She grabbed her bag and stood to walk away. As she did, she saw a policeman descending the steps into the park. For a second she froze. Then she turned to walk in the opposite direction. The boys followed her.

"You're a runaway, ain't you?" one of them asked.

Dakota kept walking.

"Look! Here comes a cop!" he yelled.

Dakota took off running and the boys ran with her. She didn't get far. The policeman caught her by the arm. It was the same officer who had taken her to the Children's Center.

"Why aren't you in school?" he demanded.

Dakota looked at him but didn't say a word. She watched as the three boys disappeared into a clump of trees.

"Oh never mind," he said as he escorted her to the squad car.

This time they did not head for the Center. As they rode along, Dakota stared out the window. When he turned onto Main street she asked, "Where are we going?"

"Well, look at that," he said. "She talks!"

"So…where are you taking me?"

The officer didn't answer but turned into a narrow alley behind a tall building. He parked the car and as they entered through a back door of the building, Dakota knew where they were.

Rejoice in hope, be patient in tribulation, be constant in prayer. Romans 12:12

CHAPTER EIGHT

"Am I under arrest?" Dakota asked.

"Not yet!" The officer pushed her into the holding cell.

"Then why are you putting me in jail?" she screamed at him.

"To keep you safe."

The judge leaned back in his oversized leather chair. Removing his glasses he addressed the people crowding the small room. "So. What do we do with her?" It was not a courtroom. It was the judge's chambers. The decision the judge was about to make would affect Dakota for the rest of her life.

Madge Denning sat on the edge of her seat. Miss Geneva stood near the door and since Mary couldn't sit still, she stood shifting her weight from foot to foot. The policeman stood behind Judge

Brown waiting for a decision. Dakota's case worker sat beside him.

Madge and Mary began to speak at the same time. The judge raised both hands and commanded, "Stop! Miss Denning, you go first."

Madge squirmed. "Okay, Judge. I have tried and tried to get Dakota to act right. I have fussed at her and even spanked her but she will not mind me. All she does is run away and live on the streets. I think it's time to put her in reform school." It was obvious the statement Madge made had been rehearsed.

"Oh no!" Mary spoke. "Please don't do that. Dakota will mind me. I can keep her safe. I can keep her in school. Please just give me the chance."

"How are you related to the child?" the judge asked Mary.

"She is not related!" Madge spat angrily. "She is a nosy old woman trying to take Dakota away from me!"

"That's enough, Miss Denning!"

The judge looked at Mary waiting for an answer.

"I'm not a relative, your Honor, but I've loved Dakota all her life.

Judge Brown looked at the case worker. "Do you have anything to say?"

"I agree with the mother. This girl stays on the streets more than anywhere else. She is a habitual runaway. A little time in the girls' school in Columbia will go a long way with this one."

Judge Brown clasped his hands together and

sighed. He looked at the officer. "You will provide the transportation?"

"Yes, your Honor."

"Oh, no! Judge please…" Mary began.

"My decision has been made, ma'am."

"May I see her before she goes?" Mary asked.

"Just long enough to say your good-bye's," he told her. He instructed Miss Geneva to produce Dakota's belongings and asked Madge to wait to sign the paperwork.

Mary hurried across the street to where Dakota sat slumped over in the holding cell. "Dakota."

Mary's voice brought Dakota to life. She jumped up from the bench and ran to Mary. The bars separated them. "Mama Mary." She laid her head against the bars reaching through them to hug Mary to her.

"They will only let me stay for a minute, Dakota. Just long enough to say good-bye."

"Good-bye?" Dakota whispered.

"Yes," Mary told her. "They are sending you to a school in Columbia. I don't know how long you will be there."

"But,"…Dakota began.

"Shhh," Mary said. "Let me finish. I only have a minute." Mary kissed Dakota's forehead through the bars. "Always remember this, Dakota. I will fight for you, I promise. I love you with all my heart. I will pray for you and angels will be watching over you, no matter where you are."

A policeman appeared. "Okay, ma'am. Time to go."

"I love you, Mama Mary."

"I love you too, sweetheart."

The ride to Columbia was a long one. Dakota had never been so far from home. Whenever the car slowed down, people would stare at the little girl in the police car. Dakota was scared. She didn't know what to expect but she took Mary's words with her.

The car stopped at a tall, double-gated entrance. Dakota read the iron words above the entrance...*South Carolina School For Girls*. Peering through the gate she saw several buildings. Four of them were dormitories - one resembled a large mansion and there were several outbuildings. But the first thing she noticed was a ten foot tall chain link fence surrounding all of it. The officer rang the buzzer and waited for the gate to open.

"This doesn't look like any school I've ever seen," she told him.

"Believe me, it's not," the officer replied.

Giant oaks lined each side of the driveway creating a canopy of leaves. The man drove slowly to the building resembling a mansion. "They call this *the big house*," he informed.

They entered the house and waited in the foyer. The entrance was as large as any room Dakota had ever seen. Scrolled wood outlined the ceiling giving it a fancy antiquated look. A seven-layered chandelier graced the center of the room.

Soon a woman appeared. She was small in stature and her gray hair was pulled back into a bun. "Hello," she said. "My name is Gladys Freling. How may I help you?"

"I have a delivery for you. Here is her paperwork."

Mrs. Freling looked over the paperwork and her wrinkles seemed to deepen. "Thank you," she said. "I will take her to Mrs. Rodderick now."

"Good luck, kid." The officer turned to go. "I'll leave your suitcase on the front steps."

As much as Dakota hated being in the custody of the policeman, she hated to see him go. He was at the very least a familiar face.

"Um, Sir...what do I do now?"

"Just hang in there, kid. You'll be okay."

Mrs. Freling touched the girl's shoulder. "Come with me, child."

Dakota obediently followed the frail woman. She noticed a disfiguring hump on the woman's back and thought she must be in a lot of pain.

Poor lady. No wonder she doesn't smile.

The office they entered looked completely out of place in the old home. The room was modern and mostly filled with file cabinets. Behind the oversized brown desk sat a middle-aged woman. She looked up as Mrs. Freling and Dakota entered the room.

Dakota fidgeted nervously with her hair as she took in her surroundings. Then her gaze settled on Mrs. Rodderick. She was a robust, stout woman, her expression stern. Her forehead had permanent frown lines and Dakota could not imagine a smile on the woman's face. Her eyes were as black as her hair and her hair as black as her mood. Dakota got the distinct impression she was a snob.

"Stand still, child," Mrs. Freling admonished her. "This is Mrs. Rodderick. She is the administrator of the school. She's in charge of your stay here and she will not put up with any foolishness."

Dakota stood at attention. *If she's in charge,* she thought. *she's the one I must become friends with. Maybe she can get me out of here.*

"Thank you, Mrs. Freling. I will let you know when we are done."

Mrs. Rodderick looked Dakota over. She first noticed the long, lanky immature body of a pre-teen. Then she saw the intelligence in the deep brown eyes. The intelligence and the sadness.

"So," Mrs. Rodderick began, "tell me why you are here, um, what is the name - Dakota?" She fingered the pages in the girl's file and offered her a seat.

Dakota sat down as she answered the question. "I don't know."

The woman looked at her incredulously. "You don't know why you're here?"

"No, ma'am."

"Well, usually girls have gotten into some kind of trouble before they are brought here." Mrs.

Rodderick waited for a response. There was none. "So, what kind of trouble did you get into?"

Dakota thought for a moment. "I ran away," she mumbled.

"Why?" asked Mrs. Rodderick.

"It's a long story," replied Dakota.

"You'll have to tell me about it sometime," the woman said. She stood abruptly, went to the door, and called for Mrs. Freling.

Mrs. Freling was right. The administrator did not put up with any foolishness. She realized immediately Dakota was testing her.

"Take Dakota to building two, please," Mrs. Rodderick said. "Have March show Dakota around."

Dakota retrieved her bag and stood on the steps of the Big House looking at four identical buildings facing her. Each dormitory was made of red brick and had a large wooden porch. From the circular drive in front of the mansion a sidewalk webbed out to each dorm.

"Come along," Mrs. Freling said. "You will be staying in the second building." The woman rang the doorbell and Dakota could hear jangling keys as they turned the lock on the other side of the door.

This is not a school, thought the girl. *This is a prison.* When the door opened, Dakota was face to face with the biggest woman she had ever seen. She was not overweight. She was just big!

"March, this is Dakota Denning. She'll be staying with us for a while. Mrs. Rodderick wants you to give her the grand tour. Dakota, this is March. She's the housemother for this building. She'll tell you all you need to know." With that said, she turned to leave.

Dakota looked at March closely. The woman had a large unattractive face. No makeup. Big ears. Her dress was a sack that came down to mid-shin and held two roomy pockets. She smiled a big toothy grin and Dakota knew immediately she was going to like her.

"Okay then," March said, "put your stuff down here and come with me." As they walked, March explained that the Big House was in the middle of the grounds. "Everything else is in a circle around it," she told her. They began their walk to the right. Crossing the driveway they stopped at a small building that looked like a log cabin. "This is the canteen," March said. "Do you have any money?"

Dakota pulled from her pants pocket the ten dollars she had saved from lunch allowance. "This is all I have."

March unlocked the canteen door and they stepped inside. "Would you like to open an account?" March asked her. "As you can see, we have soda, chips and candy and you can shop here on Saturday's."

"I don't know," Dakota said. "Is there a pay phone?"

"Oh, no," March told her. "There are no phone privileges here."

Dakota grimaced and handed March the money. The woman opened the ledger on the counter and gave Dakota a ten dollar credit.

Consider it pure joy, my brothers and sister, whenever you face trials of many kinds, because you know that the testing of your faith produces perseverance. Let perseverance finish its work so that you may be mature and complete, not lacking anything. James 1:2-4

CHAPTER NINE

They continued their tour and passed a man in a dark blue uniform.

"Good afternoon, Mr. Spellman," March said. The man tipped his hat.

"Are the police here all the time?" Dakota asked.

"Oh, he isn't a policeman. He's a security guard. There's always one on duty.

Great, thought Dakota as she eyed the fence.

"The one that patrols at night is Mr. Watts. They're both nice." March stopped to open the door to a long block building. "This is the dining room," she said. "You'll be having your meals here three times a day."

Dakota walked in to see several rows of tables lined up end to end. The bright metal and plastic chairs were of every color in the rainbow. There were no people in the room but the smell of baking bread wafted from the kitchen area. There were stacks and stacks of brown trays. *Three meals a day*, thought Dakota. *Well, that's one thing.*

March interrupted her thoughts. "Let's step outside. I'll show you the dinner bell."

The dinner bell was a black iron monstrosity about four feet tall.

"When the meal bell rings you can hear it all over the property," March told her. "You have to walk in line to meals and to and from school or the canteen. If it's not meal time it's an emergency bell and we'll tell you what to do after you line up." They continued their walk further behind the dining hall. "This building is the school. You'll meet your teachers tomorrow. You'll study the three R's...*reading, writing and arithmetic.* You'll also have a home economics class that will teach you to cook and clean."

"I could *teach* that class," Dakota interrupted.

March continued, "There's a gym class for exercise and a social hour where you'll learn how to get along with those around you."

"Social hour? You're kidding, right?"

March smiled a big toothy grin and patted the girl on the back. "Nope. Not kiddin'!" She pivoted to return to the dormitory.

"What is that building over there?" asked Dakota.

"Oh, that's the laundry," replied March. "The laundry and solitaire. We send all the sheets and towels there to be washed. You'll wash your clothes at the dorm."

"What is solitaire?"

March frowned. "Some of the kids call it lock down. It's where the troublemakers go until they can behave themselves. Just follow the rules and stay out of trouble and you won't have to worry about that building. There's one more we haven't come to yet - the Chapel. We don't have church every Sunday. Only when a preacher volunteers."

Dakota spent the next several weeks learning the rules and adjusting to the school's routine. Except for weekends, every day was pretty much the same. Get dressed - breakfast - school - lunch - school - dinner - shower - bed. Usually there were a few minutes between shower and bed to play cards or make friends, but Dakota was not interested. She had turned inward and lived in her own little world.

It was on a Saturday afternoon when the lady from church visited. Saturday's were usually spent watching TV and going to the canteen for snacks. March had told the girls on Friday someone was coming. Her name was Mrs. Grayson. She was a soft spoken lady and reminded Dakota of Mama Mary. She liked her at once. The woman came bearing gifts. The gift was a paperback New International Version of the Bible's New Testament.

"Thank you," Dakota said as she accepted her

gift.

"I have something else for you girls," Mrs. Grayson said. "A challenge. I challenge each of you to memorize the entire book of Philippians found in this New Testament."

A low murmur spread throughout the crowd of girls.

"I know what you are thinking," Mrs. Grayson said. "But it really is not more than you can handle. It's only four chapters."

Some of the girls said, *"no thanks,"* and went to sit on the swings in the yard of the dorm. A few stayed to hear what else Mrs. Grayson had to say.

"I will come back in one month to see who has memorized the whole Book. If you do, I will present you with a hardback copy of the entire Bible. Whenever you leave here you can keep it for yourself or you'll have a nice gift for someone on the outside."

Dakota wanted that Bible. She thought about how proud Mama Mary would be and she wanted to give the Bible as a gift to her. So, Dakota accepted the challenge and began reading the book of Philippians immediately.

The next day a preacher came by and the girls went to Chapel. Mrs. Grayson was there and the preacher spoke on the Book of Philippians. He explained how it was a letter of joy written by someone named Paul. He told them Paul was in prison when he wrote it. He had been imprisoned because he was a Christian and was writing a *thank you letter* to the people of Philippi for their gift of love.

Dakota found the story interesting and thought it might help her to memorize the verses. She also thought about how it felt to be in prison. She knew she was in a school, but it felt more like prison. Dakota worked hard at memorizing the four chapters and after one month four of the girls were ready to recite them to Mrs. Grayson.

Dakota received her Bible.

"I'm so proud of you, Dakota," March told her. "I have another reward for you. Claudia is going home tomorrow. You'll take her place as trustee."

Trustee was a much desired position among the girls. There were only two in each building - one on each end of the long hallway. A trustee always led the line of girls wherever they went. She was the one to check the girls' doors at night to be sure they were locked but her door could remain open. There were many perks to being a trustee.

The Christmas season came and with it came several days of celebration. Church visitors brought bags of fruit, nuts and candy canes to every girl. There was singing of carols and even a play put on by a few of the older girls at school. Christmas Eve was designated visitation day for the families of the girls. Dakota spent the day in her room alone.

March stopped by to check on her. "No visitors, huh?"

"My Mama would not come this far just to see me", Dakota said, "and she won't let Mama Mary come see me. But that's okay." Dakota tried to sound brave.

"No," March said. "It's not okay, Dakota. Everyone should have visitors for Christmas."

On Christmas morning, March called to Dakota to wake up. "Merry Christmas! Time to wake the girls."

Dakota stretched and rolled out of bed. She looked around the small gray room. A bed, a dresser with a chair and a chest of drawers was all there was.

It doesn't look like Christmas and it doesn't feel like Christmas, she thought. But then most of her Christmases were that way.

She dressed quickly and walked down the hall opening doors as she went. "Merry Christmas, Tish." And a little farther. "Wake up, Carla. Merry Christmas."

Soon everyone was awake and the breakfast bell was ringing.

There was a collective gasp as the girls from the different dormitories entered the dining hall. A twenty foot spruce pine complete with lights, tinsel and a star stood in the middle of the room. There were hundreds of gifts under the tree and a record player filled the air with Christmas music.

Dakota had never seen such a sight. She picked up a tray and realized the usual oatmeal breakfast had been replaced with bacon and French toast. There were apples and oranges and ice cold milk. The girls were given extra time to finish their meal.

Mrs. Rodderick went to stand near the tree to address them. "Good morning and Merry Christmas..." she began. "After you return your dishes and trays, please return to your seats."

Once everyone was seated, the housemothers began handing out the gifts. Listening to the girls chatter, Dakota soon realized the gifts were from their families back home. *Well,* Dakota thought, *guess there won't be any gifts for me.*

Just then, March placed the biggest box of all in front of Dakota. The wrapping was red with green Christmas trees and ribbon. It was full of wrapped packages. "We couldn't let her in to see you," March whispered, "but I did get special permission to deliver her gift."

After giving March a hug, Dakota opened the envelope attached to the box and read through her tears. "My dear, sweet Dakota. I wish I could see you this Christmas day. I miss you so much and worry about you being there. I hope you like the presents I brought you and I hope the clothes fit. I baked you a pineapple cake to share with the girls in your dorm. Merry Christmas, Dakota. Don't forget...there are angels watching over you always. We love you and we pray for you every day." The card was signed,

Mama Mary and Big Daddy.

Dakota looked up at March. "The cake is at the dorm," March said.

Dakota smiled as the tears fell. "Did you meet her?" she asked March. "Was she here?" March shook her head, yes.

"She came all this way?"

"Yes," said March. "She knew she couldn't come in to see you, but she came all this way so you could have a good Christmas." March was glad she brought the gifts in to Dakota. She could get into trouble for doing it but seeing the smile on Dakota's face was worth it.

I can do everything through Him Who gives me strength. Philippians 4:13

CHAPTER TEN

That evening after the girls' doors were closed for the night, March called Dakota to the small pantry inside the dorm. "I thought you might like to have a piece of the cake you got this morning. You can share with the girls tomorrow."

Dakota smiled. She had been smiling all day. The box from Mama Mary contained the biggest teddy bear yet, a navy skirt and white blouse, a cross necklace, toiletries, and money for the canteen. But Dakota was starved for affection of any kind and the note reminding her she was loved was what meant the most to her.

"I would love to have some cake but only if you have a piece too."

March and Dakota carried their treat into the common room.

"Why don't you tell me about Mama Mary?"

"Well, I've known Mama Mary and Big Daddy since I was just a little baby. She was best friends with my mama. But my mama messed that up."

"How did she mess it up?" March asked.

"My mama wanted to be Big Daddy's girlfriend and Big Daddy told her *no*. So that made my mama mad. Of course, everything makes my mama mad. If you ask me, Mama Mary is the one who should have been mad. But she just said she was glad Big Daddy did the right thing. After that I didn't get to see Mama Mary much."

March leaned in to whisper, "You love her very much, don't you?"

"Oh, yes! I miss her something awful."

Christmas was a good day for Dakota but beginning the day after, things began to change. Several of the girls on Dakota's end of the building had tried to become friends with her. She had rejected their offers of friendship. Now it seemed she turned inward even more. Slowly her situation began to make her angry.

Spring came early. Whole families came to visit most of the girls and they filled the yards of the dorms. Dakota began to frown and stare at the visitors making them uncomfortable.

"What is wrong with that girl?" asked one of the visitors. A blue eyed girl named Marcie spoke up. "Don't pay her any attention. She's weird. Keeps to herself most of the time. Never has visitors. She's probably just jealous."

Dakota heard what the girl said. *Marcie is right*, she thought. *I am jealous.*

March began to notice the change in Dakota. She took note of the moodiness and reported her concerns to Mrs. Rodderick.

"Keep an eye on her," Mrs. Rodderick told March. "If you think I should talk to her, let me know. We don't want this to get out of hand."

School was back in session. Dakota was an average student that could do better when she wanted to. She didn't care for most of her classes but she loved to write and she loved history. Today she had home economics class and she simply was not interested.

"Dakota!" the teacher admonished her. "Are you paying attention?"

"No," she replied.

"Why not?"

"I don't know," the girl said and crossed her arms defiantly.

This surprised the teacher. Dakota has been a quiet, uninterested student but never disrespectful.

"Please pay attention," the teacher requested.

"Nope," replied Dakota.

The teacher sat down at her desk and wrote for a few minutes. She handed the note to one of the other girls and asked her to take it to Mrs. Rodderick. A few minutes later, the girl re-appeared with Mr. Spellman.

"What's the trouble?" the security guard asked.

"Please escort Dakota Denning to Mrs. Rodderick's office." She handed another note to him as he and Dakota started for the door.

"What is going on with you, Dakota? This is the second person to voice concern over your behavior. Care to tell me about it?" Mrs. Rodderick was pacing back and forth.

"I don't want to be here," Dakota replied. "All the other girls spend visitation day laughing and talking with their families while I sit in my room staring at the walls."

"Or staring at the visitors?"

Dakota shifted in her seat.

Mrs. Rodderick paced some more. Finally she asked, "Dakota, would you like to see your mother and siblings?"

"No!" Dakota was quick to reply. "Well, maybe my brothers and sister. And Mama Mary."

"But not your mother?"

"My *real* mother?"

"Yes."

"No, ma'am. I would not like to see her."

"Why not?" Mrs. Rodderick was getting frustrated.

"I just wouldn't. That's all."

Dakota was still too scared of Mama to tell anyone in authority how she was treated.

"Why are you so mad at your mother?"

Dakota didn't answer.

"Are we through talking, Dakota?"

"Yes."

"Yes, what?"

"Yes, ma'am."

With that said and done, Mrs. Rodderick called for Mr. Spellman.

"Take her to March. Tell March I would like to speak to her."

The housemother was surprised to see Dakota back early. Since she was sent back as punishment, her door had to be locked for the day. It was unusual to lock in a trustee but March did not take away that privilege.

"I could make someone else trustee," March told Dakota, "but I believe in second chances. I hope you won't let me down again."

That evening the door to Dakota's room was left unlocked. After the girls were in bed March knocked at Dakotas door.

"Dakota, come to the common room, please. I would like to talk to you."

Dakota followed March wondering, *what now?*

March spoke. "Because we're a part of the juvenile justice system, we have to read all of the mail that comes in. Sometimes we give the mail to the girls, but other times, for various reasons, we withhold it."

Dakota's face lit up. "Mail?" she asked.

84

"Yes," March replied. "You received a letter a while back. I couldn't give it to you without permission from the judge who signed you in here.

"Why?"

March pulled the letter from her pocket and offered it to Dakota.

"Because it's from your Mama Mary."

Dakota took in a sharp breath and carefully opened the letter.

March stood back and left the girl with her joy.

My dearest Dakota,

I am praying you will get this letter because I am afraid if not, you will think I have forgotten you. I wish so much that I could see you and hug you and tell you how much I miss you. The housemother there has written me to tell me how well you are doing and that you are memorizing Bible verses. I am so proud of you. I also wanted to tell you that Big Daddy and I have applied through the state to become foster parents to any children that need our love. We are caring for a baby boy right now. He is very sick but oh so sweet. But don't you worry, Dakota. No one will ever take your place. There is a place in my heart that will always be reserved for you and no one else. I love you and remember God's angels are watching over you.

Love, Mama Mary

Dakota folded the letter and placed it back in the

envelope. There were so many emotions jumbled up at once - joy, fear, jealousy. It had been ten months since she had seen Mama Mary. She was ecstatic to hold a letter in her hand. Except for Christmas, this was the only time she had heard from anyone. But now she felt the jealousy of Mama Mary and Big Daddy loving another child - a boy. Fear began to set in. *What if they love him more than me?* Dakota wanted to leave now more than ever.

The next day was Saturday. After breakfast, the girls had cleaning chores and all was normal until March came to talk to Dakota. "Mrs. Rodderick wants to see me. Everything should be fine without me for a few minutes." March reached into the pocket of the shift she wore. "For safety reasons someone has to have a key to open the doors." March unlocked the front door and turned to hand the keys to Dakota. "I won't be long," she said.

Dakota returned to where she was buffing the wax on the long hallway floor. She looked left, then right. There were doors at both ends of the hall. The girls never used these doors only the front door. Now Dakota looked at the keys in her hand, then at the closest door. Walking down the hallway, she checked to see if the girls were in their rooms. One by one, she told them it was time for midday rest and shut their doors.

She went into the showers to get Marcie and Tish. "Rest period," she told them. "You can finish cleaning later." Once all the girls were in their rooms Dakota went to the end of the hallway. Her heart began to pound and with sweaty hands she fumbled with the keys until she heard the lock turn. Bursting through the door, Dakota ran like she had never run before.

See that you do not despise one of these little ones. For I tell you that their angels in heaven always see the face of my Father in heaven. Matthew 18:10

CHAPTER ELEVEN

Dakota didn't realize the hall doors had alarms and the wailing of the loud alarm made her run even faster. *Whoo! Whoo! Whoo! Whoo!* The alarm seemed to get louder. That and her heartbeat was all she could hear swooshing in her ears. *If I can get over the fence they will never catch me*, she thought. The chain link fence shook and rattled as Dakota grabbed the honeycombed metal.

Halfway up the fence she felt two strong hands around her waist pulling her hard to the ground. "Whoa, Missy," Mr. Spellman yelled. He had a death grip on her wrist and was pulling her along behind him. Dakota struggled to get free but soon realized it was useless.

Mr. Spellman stopped by the dorm to pick up the keys Dakota had thrown down once she was outside. He used one of the keys to silence the alarm. He slammed the door and headed for Mrs. Rodderick's office with Dakota in tow. March, Mrs. Rodderick and Mrs. Freling heard the alarm and met them in the driveway. All of them wore a frown.

"I pulled her off the fence," Mr. Spellman told them.

Mrs. Rodderick looked at Mrs. Freling and nodded toward the laundry building. "You know what to do," she said.

The short matronly woman acknowledged her request and asked Mr. Spellman to bring Dakota along.

The three of them entered the whitewashed block building. Dakota smelled the detergent used to clean the linens and saw steam coming from a room to her left.

Mr. Spellman led Dakota through a door and into a long, dark corridor. They stopped for a moment to adjust to the low lighting. The air was cold, damp and musty. A moment later Mrs. Freling came in behind them with keys jingling in her hand.

As the woman opened a large heavy door, Dakota found the courage to speak.

"What is this place?" she asked.

"Lockdown," Mrs. Freling answered.

Dakota took in a cold breath. "How long will I be here?"

"That depends on you and Mrs. Rodderick."

Behind the heavy door there was another door. It was made of iron bars. The scraping and squeaking sound it made as it was opened echoed through the dark hallway. Mr. Spellman guided Dakota into the cell. The room was twelve feet deep. Nine feet wide. Dakota noticed a small square window up near the ceiling. It let in little light. It, too, had bars and the glass had long been broken out.

Dakota jumped at the sound of the doors closing behind her. She heard the key clicking the lock into place. Then silence... Turning, she grabbed the bars and yelled to Mrs. Freling. "I have more questions!"

Stillness. Silence.

Hot tears began to slowly ride to the cold tiled floor. There was a wooden cot anchored to the wall under the window. Dakota picked up the rolled up thin mattress and unfurled it onto the hard planks. Inside the mattress she found a washcloth and towel. That was when Dakota realized the only other things in the room were a sink and a toilet. Dakota sat on the cot. She pulled her knees up to her chin, leaned against the cold cement wall, and continued to cry.

Hours passed before Dakota heard the rattle in the heavy solid door. When it opened, she saw Mrs. Freling had returned. The woman held a tray with a peanut butter sandwich and a metal cup with milk in it. "I have your meal for the day," she said. "From now on, that's what you'll get - one meal a day. You may keep this cup so you can get water from the sink." She passed the tray under the door made of bars. It scraped on the tiling of the floor. Mrs. Freling shoved a gray nightgown between the bars and told Dakota to take it. "Give me your clothes and put this on," she told the girl. "You may keep your underwear but you'll need to wash it out by hand. I'll bring you a clean gown two times a week."

Dakota was embarrassed to undress in front of the woman. She turned her back to make the change. "I have a radio in my room," Dakota said. "Can I have it in here?"

She handed her clothes to Mrs. Freling as the woman replied, "No. You are being punished." With that the door was closed again.

The next morning Dakota awoke to the sound of the breakfast bell and soon heard children's voices in the distance. She was cold and wrapped the towel around her like a shawl. After a while the silence began to hurt her ears. She tried humming and then began reciting the book of Philippians over and over again. This was something she would continue to do day after day for weeks. She took strength from the verses and felt a peace she did not understand.

Dakota longed to talk to Mama Mary and fantasized how it would be to go home to her. She was jealous to know she would have to share Mama Mary with a little boy but knew in her heart that Mama Mary had enough love to give them both.

After four nights had passed, Dakota was startled by a voice outside the cell window. It was a man's voice. There came a loud whisper. "Hey!

Little girl! You awake?"

Dakota rolled up the mattress and stood on it. She stretched on her tiptoes trying to look out the small window. It was pitch black.

"Who's out there?" she asked him.

"Night watchman. Name's Watts but the girls call me Hershey." Mr. Watts continued in a loud whisper. "Want to know why they call me Hershey?"

"Sure," Dakota said.

"Okay. Step back, away from the window."

Dakota jumped off the cot and heard something hit the mattress. A sliver of moonlight pierced the dark and she saw a chocolate bar on the bed. It was the first time she had smiled in a long time. Dakota grabbed the candy and jumped back up to thank the man.

"You're welcome," he said. "Now what's your name and how'd you get in there?"

Over the next several weeks, Mr. Watts brought Dakota a candy bar every time he came to work. He reminded her often to be sure and flush the wrappers. They talked in whispers about her life and his.

Dakota never saw Mr. Watts but she was grateful to him, and for him. She sometimes wondered if he was one of the guardian angels Mama Mary promised would be watching over her.

The hours and days dragged by. Thirty days passed and Dakota heard the key. It was not time for her daily meal so she was surprised when Mrs. Freling opened both doors. "Here are your clothes," the woman said. "Get dressed and come with me."

Dakota didn't speak but did as she was told. She followed Mrs. Freling through the building and out into the sunlight. It was so bright Dakota squinted and shielded her eyes with her hand. The warmth felt wonderful. She wished she could stand there for a while.

"Come along, Dakota. Don't dawdle."

Entering the big house, Dakota dreaded seeing Mrs. Rodderick. She went into the woman's office and stood in front of her desk waiting for her to look up. Mrs. Rodderick began to talk while looking at papers in a folder.

"This procedure is very simple, Dakota. It is your parole hearing."

Dakota shifted her weight from her left foot to her right.

"Stand up straight!" barked Mrs. Rodderick.

Then the woman stood. She looked at Dakota and said, "I have one simple question for you. Are you ready to go home?"

Dakota looked her squarely in the eye and answered her question with a question, "Is home with my real mother?"

"Yes," Mrs. Rodderick answered.

"Then, no. I won't go!"

The woman could not believe what she was hearing. "Why not?" she asked her.

Dakota answered, "I want to live with Mama Mary."

Mrs. Rodderick slammed the folder shut and said, "Thirty more days!"

As soon as Dakota was back in the cell, she curled up on the cot and fell asleep. Sleep was still her escape and her depression granted her plenty. Day after day, the loneliness defined her hours. The hunger inflicted the physical pain while the mental anguish came from counting the days. Dakota stopped reciting Philippians and began talking to God. Most of the time her talks began with *Why?* There were a few incidents she didn't acknowledge Mr. Watts and kept quiet when he called her name. He seemed to understand and tossed her a candy bar inside anyhow knowing she would find it.

You will seek me and find me when you seek me with all your heart. Jeremiah 29:13

CHAPTER TWELVE

Thirty days passed and Dakota once again was taken before Mrs. Rodderick. The outcome was the same. *Thirty more days.* Dakota was deflated. The longer she stayed in lockdown, the more bitter she became.

After three months of being shut away and half starved, Dakota was barely recognizable. She was pale and gaunt. She needed food. She needed sunshine. Today would be the third time she would go for possibility of parole. Dakota had been at the school for fourteen months and her spirit was broken. She put on her clothes for the walk to the mansion. It was the same outfit she had received from Mama Mary for Christmas. It had fit her perfectly. It was a silky white blouse and navy blue a-line skirt. Now, she held on to the skirt at the waist line because if she let go it would fall down around her ankles. Even Mrs. Rodderick was concerned when she saw how frail Dakota had become. The light had gone from her eyes and the fight was gone from her body.

"Are you ready to go home now?" Mrs. Rodderick dreaded to hear the answer.

Meekly, Dakota whispered, "Yes."

Mrs. Rodderick asked the guard to take Dakota to her dorm. She told her she would have to wait until her social worker could be contacted but she would be leaving that day.

Dakota was glad to be leaving lockdown but could not get excited about leaving. She dreaded going home to Mama.

March welcomed her with open arms and could not believe how emaciated the girl had become. Dakota's room had long since been given to someone else so March took her into her private quarters. She retrieved the girl's belongings from the hall closet and placed them next to Dakota. "Find something to wear," she told her.

Dakota dug through the box and found the smallest outfit. She touched the radio Mama Mary had sent her and hugged the hard-earned Bible to her chest. After removing all she would need to wear home, she pushed the box of belongings toward March. "You can give this stuff to some of the girls," she said. "My Mama will just throw it all away." She left to take a long, hot shower. When returning, she knocked on the house mother's open door - her hair wet in a towel.

"Come in, Dakota."

She entered the room and sat as she had before.

March had a food tray waiting for her.

Dakota drank the soup and milk, although almost too tired to eat. She addressed March as she brushed her hair. "Why are you being so nice to me? You trusted me with your keys and I tried to run."

March smiled at her as she answered, "I would have thought your Mama Mary had taught you all about forgiveness, Dakota."

"Thank you," Dakota replied.

Four hours later, Mama came to get Dakota. She had Stevie, Brenden and Alysa with her. All of the children hugged Dakota and were happy to see her. Alysa was shy about it. Mama didn't hug her. Mama just told her to get in the back seat with the boys.

Dakota did as she was told and curled up in the corner and went to sleep. She had to hold back the tears when the car pulled into the driveway. The first thing she saw was the shed and she already dreaded the nights she would be taken there. The depression that already had a grip on Dakota, now deepened. She politely told the younger children she was tired and didn't want to play.

As she entered the small house, she was surprised to find Granny there. "I'm here to visit for a while," she said.

Dakota thought it strange that Granny was visiting for more than a day but she was happy about it. She knew Mama wouldn't hurt her as long as Granny was there and she made Dakota's return bearable. She watched the children and did the cooking. She recognized the depression in Dakota and nurtured the girl as much as she knew how.

Mama kept her distance and didn't have much to say to her. Dakota figured out that Granny being there was the social worker's idea. Mama still left every evening and this was when Dakota healed. Granny would cook supper and the children laughed, talked, and went to bed happy.

However, after a week when Granny told them it was time for her to go home, they became sad - especially Dakota. "Please take me with you," Dakota begged. "Please, Granny, let me come stay with you."

"Now, you know your Mama won't let you do that, Dakota. She needs you to help with the little ones," Granny said. "Tonight is my last night here and I have to go check on your Grandpa. I'll bet he's ready for me to cook him some biscuits." Granny smiled and patted Dakota's shoulder.

Life returned to the way it had been for years for Dakota. Barely thirteen, she felt like and began to look like an adult. She cooked and scrubbed and did laundry and took care of the children. She took beatings when Mama had a bad day.

Rocky was spending more and more time at T.J.'s house or at Aunt Hettie's, so Dakota had no help. But Rocky was home today and she still didn't get everything done Mama had asked her to do. When Mama looked for the clean laundry, Dakota closed her eyes and groaned.

"I need my black dress, Dakota. Where is it?" Mama asked her.

"I haven't washed it yet," Dakota replied.

"What?" Mama was immediately infuriated. "I need that dress!" she screamed at Dakota.

"I'm sorry, Mama."

Mama mocked her, *"I'm sorry, Mama. I didn't mean to, Mama. Please forgive me, Mama.* I am about tired of your sorrys!" She called to Rocky and he came running. "Go outside," she ordered. "Bring me a stick."

Rocky ran out the door and soon returned with a hickory switch.

"I don't want that switch," Mama said. "I want a *stick!*"

Rocky went out again and returned with a small branch from the oak tree behind the house.

"I'm giving you one more chance to get it right, Rocky."

"Yes ma'am," he replied. Rocky returned a few minutes later with the *stick* - a 3'x3"x3" piece of wood from the neighbor's garage repair stash. It was long, sturdy and square with four sharp edges.

"Get on your knees, Dakota," Mama ordered.

"Mama...please..."

"Shut up, Dakota. Get on your knees!"

Dakota did as she was told.

Whack! The first blow took the breath from her. Dakota tried to stand but Mama pushed her back to her knees.

Whack! Dakota felt blood trickle down her back. Again, she tried to stand, just as the third blow crossed the side of her throat.

Mama grabbed Dakota's arm and twisting it hard brought her back to the floor.

Whack! This one caught her arm and tore the sleeve of her shirt. Dakota pitched forward, catching herself on all fours.

Rocky tried to yell above Mama's yelling and Dakota's crying.

"Mama!" he said. "Mama! She's had enough!"

Mama turned to yell at Rocky and chase him out the front door.

Dakota jumped up from the floor and ran out the back door silently thanking her brother for saving her life. She knew all the short cuts and dark places. She knew she had to hide or Mama would beat her to death.

The next morning, Dakota stood on Mama Mary's front porch ringing the doorbell. She had walked all night to get there. Tired, cold, hungry, and hurting, she fell into Mary's arms. She had not seen her in over a year and was overjoyed to finally be there.

"Dakota!" Mary whispered. "Oh, dear Lord, come in, child."

She flinched when Mary hugged her.

Mary could see the welt on the side of Dakota's throat and blood staining her shirt. She carefully lifted the girl's shirt to see the swollen cuts and dried blood on her back. "Oh, my poor baby," Mary said. "Come sit down. You're shivering. I'll get you a blanket." She wrapped it around Dakota and went to call the police.

"You've asked them to send a deputy," Dakota said. "You can't send me back. She'll kill me," she began to cry.

"I'm not sending you back, Dakota. I'm reporting a *crime*!"

While waiting for the police to come, Mary scrambled some eggs for Dakota to eat and made her hot chocolate.

The policeman arrived and Mary told him what happened. She lifted Dakota's shirt to show the officer.

"I am now a licensed *Foster Parent for the State*," Mary told him. "I want to keep this child in my custody until a court hearing can be arranged. I'll take her to the doctor this morning and have her injuries checked."

The officer called to clear it with his superior. Dakota was allowed to stay.

Mary made some more calls that day. The

hearing was scheduled for the next afternoon.

Mary and Dakota left early for the Family Court hearing. They parked behind the white six-story building.

"I've got butterflies," Dakota said.

"Me, too," admitted Mary. "But I've come prepared and prayed most of the night. You're going to be fine." Mary didn't tell Dakota she had been keeping a journal. She wrote down all the times Dakota had run away and why. She took Polaroid pictures of Dakota's injuries and she had a doctor's statement. Mary wanted the judge to see the items of proof before the hearing - their reason for arriving early. Besides, she didn't want to risk running into Madge in the parking lot.

Mary and Dakota were already seated in the courtroom when Madge entered. Looks were exchanged - words were not.

An officer of the court approached Mary and Dakota. "The judge wishes to see Dakota in his chambers alone," he advised.

Wide-eyed, Dakota looked at Mary.

"Go ahead," Mary said. "It will be fine. The judge is your friend. Go talk to him."

When Dakota stood to go with the man, she saw Granny and Aunt Hettie enter the courtroom. The butterflies in her stomach doubled.

Sixty-year-old Melvin Roper sat behind a sturdy walnut desk. He had already donned his robe and was thumbing through papers. "Hello," he said as Dakota came into the room.

"Hello," she replied shyly.

"Have a seat, Dakota."

She sat down and began to nervously play with her hair.

"I have been looking at some pictures and notes that Mrs. Stockton brought me," Judge Roper said. "I have a few questions for you, then we will meet everyone else in the courtroom. Okay?"

"Yes sir," Dakota replied. A few minutes later, she returned to the courtroom. A social worker instructed Dakota to sit next to her. She longed to sit with Mary but did as she was told.

The judge entered the room and everyone stood in his honor. They returned to their seats at his gesture. He began to speak. "This hearing is to determine whether Dakota Denning will become a ward of the state or return home with her mother, Madge Denning, or be placed with another relative."

Dakota began to fidget and the social worker placed a hand on her arm to calm her.

The judge continued. "It seems I have several options from which to choose." He picked up a document. "It says here that Dakota's grandmother would like for her to come live with her. Her aunt would like to take her home as well. Then, of course, there is Mrs. Denning."

Madge stood to her feet. "Of course, I want to take her home," she said. "I don't even know why we're here. She's my daughter. I'm taking her home - no one else!"

"Sit down, Mrs. Denning," the judge ordered firmly. "Normally I would send Dakota to live with a relative if I didn't send her home with her mother. But Dakota tells me that sending her home with her grandmother or aunt would be the same as sending her home with her mother."

Madge jumped up again. "She's a kid! She don't know what she wants!" she yelled.

The judge was infuriated. "Mrs. Denning, if I have to tell you to sit down one more time, I will have you removed from the courtroom." He continued, "My judgment is to grant custody of Dakota to Mary Stockton, a foster parent of the state."

Madge jumped to her feet. "I will kill you - you idiot judge!" she yelled.

The officer of the court was immediately by her side just as she pulled a gun from her purse. He restrained her and Judge Roper continued. "I am ordering a restraining order and Mrs. Denning, you will not come within five hundred yards of the said child, Dakota Denning, or her foster parents, Mr. and Mrs. Stockton."

It took Dakota a moment to take it all in. She failed to realize she had stood up and tears were flowing. The social worker squeezed her arm and turned her to face Mary across the room. Dakota looked at Mama. She couldn't speak out loud but mouthed the words, *I forgive you.*

Mama bowed her head as Dakota ran into Mary's open arms. "Mama Mary!" the girl breathed aloud.

"From now on," Mary promised, "you can call me *Mother.*" She smiled, "Now, let's go home."

"For I know the plans I have for you," declares the Lord, "plans to prosper you and not to harm you, plans to give you hope and a future." Jeremiah 29:11

DEBORAH NORTON

EPILOGUE

Ten years later Dakota was shopping for Mama Mary's birthday dinner. *I think I will make a cheesecake for Mother this year*, she thought. She planned for Mama Mary, Big Daddy, her husband and their brand new son to celebrate at her home that night.

As she left the grocery store she froze in her tracks. A car was parked next to the sidewalk and she immediately recognized the woman behind the wheel. It was Mama!

"Hello, Dakota," Mama said.

"Hello."

"I don't want to bother you, Dakota. I won't keep you but a minute. I just wanted to tell you that I have given my heart to God. I am saved now. But I had to come tell you I am sorry for all I did to you when you were little, and I want to ask you to forgive me."

"I forgive you, Mama. I forgave you a long time ago."

"Are you happy, Dakota?"

"Yes, Mama. Very happy."

"Then I hope you stay happy and I hope you have a good life."

As Mama drove away Dakota silently thanked God for saving her Mama and thanked Him again for her loving family.

If you declare with your mouth, "Jesus is Lord," and believe in your heart that God raised him from the dead, you will be saved. For it is with your heart that you believe and are justified, and it is with your mouth that you profess your faith and are saved. Romans 10:9-10

DEBORAH NORTON

ABOUT THE AUTHOR

Deborah Norton currently resides in a small town in the upstate of South Carolina. A happy and loving mother of three and 'Nana' to many, she is passionate about life and advocates intervention whenever children are neglected or abused.

27282519R00073

Made in the USA
Charleston, SC
07 March 2014